Economic Change, Governance and Natural Resource Wealth

Bundesministerium für wirtschaftliche Zusammenarbeit
und Entwicklung

 Canadian International   **Agence canadienne de**
                       Development Agency   **developpement international**

Canadian International Development Agency

Danish Ministry of Foreign Affairs, Secretariat for the
Environment and Sustainable Development

European Commission, DG Development

Deutsche Gesellschaft für Technische Zusammenarbeit, GmbH

Swiss Agency for Development and Cooperation

Swedish International Development Cooperation Agency

The development agencies identified above provided financial support for the Macroeconomic Reform and Sustainable Development in Southern Africa project and for this publication. Their contributions do not imply responsibility for or endorsement of the analysis or recommendations offered herein.

Economic Change, Governance and Natural Resource Wealth

The Political Economy of
Change in Southern Africa

DAVID REED

earthscan
from Routledge

First published in the UK and USA in 2001 by
Earthscan Publications Ltd

This edition published 2013 by Earthscan

For a full list of publications please contact:

Earthscan
2 Park Square, Milton Park, Abingdon, Oxon OX14 4RN
Simultaneously published in the USA and Canada by Earthscan
711 Third Avenue, New York, NY 10017

Earthscan is an imprint of the Taylor & Francis Group, an informa business

ISBN: 978-1-85383-872-9 (pbk)

Typesetting by JS Typesetting, Wellingborough, Northants
Cover design by Susanne Harris

A catalogue record for this book is available from the British Library

Library of Congress Cataloging-in-Publication Data

Reed, David, 1948–.
    Economic change, governance and natural resource wealth : the political
    economy of change in southern Africa / by David Reed.
        p. cm.
    Includes bibliographical references and index.
    ISBN 1-85383-877-2 (hb) — ISBN 1-85383-872-1 (pbk.)
        1. Natural resources—Africa, Southern—Management.   2. Africa,
    Southern—Economic conditions.   I. Title.

HC900.Z65 R437 2001
333.7′0968—dc21   2001004666

Contents

List of Maps

Foreword

by Poul Nielson

Over the past decade the European Commission has supported WWF's efforts to analyze the impact of structural reforms on the environment of developing countries. More recently, the Commission joined six other development agencies in trying to influence the implementation of structural reform programmes so as to increase the attention given by governments and the Bretton Woods institutions to the environmental impacts in countries of southern Africa that rely heavily on natural resource wealth. This research and advocacy programme was carried out by WWF's Macroeconomics Program Office with local partners in countries of the region.

This endeavor to influence the implementation of the economic reform process encountered unanticipated challenges. Difficulties arose not from particular shortcomings of project partners but rather from the very character of the systems of governance and the economic arrangements that had evolved in those resource-rich countries following independence.

The essays presented in this publication explore the complex dynamics of how governments in Tanzania, Zambia and Zimbabwe sought to construct egalitarian societies using those countries' diverse natural resource wealth. They then go on to explore how the subsequent state-dominated economies and one-party political systems responded to the imperative to embark on sweeping economic changes under the guidance of the World Bank and IMF. At the heart of this book's concerns is the effort to understand the difficulties of promoting equitable, sustainable development paths in the context of resource-based economies that lack transparent and accountable systems of governance.

These essays are both insightful and troubling. They are insightful because they take a cross-disciplinary approach to understanding the complex interaction between economic and political actors, both national and international, as resource-based countries undergo structural change. They are troubling because they bring into the open numerous sensitive issues regarding power, privilege, systems of governance, corruption and, above all, the impact of these dynamics on the rural poor.

I cannot say that I embrace all the views and opinions presented by the author. Indeed, this is not a prerequisite for presenting this publication to the broader public. I do, however, want to commend these interpretative essays because they highlight the challenges that the Commission, along with the development agencies of Member States, must address if we are to hold true to our commitment to alleviate poverty and promote environmental sustainability. Foremost among those challenges is guaranteeing that the evolving economic systems in Africa and on other continents use their valuable natural resources to promote the benefit of the general public. Specifically, we must reexamine our assumptions as to whether the economic structures resulting from structural change will allow the rural poor to increase their productivity and living standards while putting in place resource management systems that will allow those benefits to flow over a sustained period of time.

Integration of the global economy guarantees that rapid change will be a permanent feature of national economic life for years to come. To be successful, countries must increase their capacity to respond to new market forces and opportunities. Yet, as this book reminds us, governments must also respond to the evolving needs of its citizens, particularly to the needs of the most vulnerable. An integral part of increasing the capacity of governments to respond to these shifting needs is forging a deeper, more substantive partnership with the many groups and institutions of civil society on which the legitimacy and credibility of governments must ultimately depend.

In this context, I agree with the author's recommendation that the European Commission and other development agencies must increase investment in strengthening the analytical, monitoring and advocacy capacity of civil society. This increased capacity is particularly important in societies that are experiencing both social and economic change with associated dangers such as uneven distribution of wealth, corruption and civil strife.

As the debate regarding the benefits and costs of globalization evolves in the coming years, I hope that the reader will use the analysis and recommendations presented in this publication as a gauge to help assess the direction of the changes unfolding around us. These essays should remind us of the inadequacy of one-dimensional analytical approaches to understanding these changes, as they will also oblige us to ensure that the poor, particularly the rural poor, in developing countries remain the beneficiaries of the changes promoted by the Commission and its partners.

Poul Nielson
Commissioner for Development Co-operation and Humanitarian Aid
European Commission

Preface

by David Kaimowitz

When I first visited Zimbabwe about 15 years ago, I found an optimistic nation looking forward to a better future. Blacks and whites mingled uneasily, but both seemed to realize that they would have to work together to promote their mutual interests. The commercial farmers were exporting lots of maize, cotton and tobacco, and the country's industries were slowly making progress. Most people I talked to expressed confidence that the government could find a way to use some of the revenue generated by those activities to improve the conditions in the shantytowns and communal areas. A cautious land reform would help redress historical injustices and provide new sources of livelihood to poor families without destroying the large commercial farm sector and the country's ability to earn foreign exchange. University professors and students earnestly debated which policies could hasten the pace of progress and were keen to learn about how to get things right. Independence made people proud and they expressed that pride with grace and dignity.

These days, that Zimbabwe seems difficult to remember. When I lasted visited Harare several months ago, I encountered quite a different place. What stands out most in my mind are the long lines of cars queuing for gasoline, the black market for dollars, the unemployed young men squatting on the country's best farms and the widespread anger over corruption and the arrogance of power. Despite budget cuts, tear gas and decaying facilities the university was subsisting but had ceased to inspire. Friends told me that the poor farmers on the communal lands were finding it nearly impossible to eke out a living and that the soils and woodlands they depended on were rapidly deteriorating.

It wasn't supposed to be like that. The government promised it would work for the people. The World Bank, the IMF and the international development agencies assured everyone that economic reform would bring prosperity. But the poor are still there for all to see. There are, in fact, more of them today than there were 15 years ago.

The easiest thing, of course, is to blame the president. One could undoubtedly think of all sorts of good reasons to do so. However, that would not explain why Zimbabwe's neighbours face similar problems. Nor would it explain how the same president went from being the darling of the international community and popular among his people to his current state of isolation. To say that one man or party has been in power too long begs the question of why that has happened and why more democratic institutions have failed to emerge.

The truth, as this publication documents, is much more complex. Most southern African countries suffer declining terms of trade. In real terms, they receive a lot less for their products today than they did several decades ago. They also receive much less international assistance now that 'trade, not aid' has become the mantra of the international development community. In some cases structural adjustment programmes and economic liberalization helped to avert economic chaos and even brought modest growth. But there is no sign that such policies will lift these countries out of poverty any time soon.

In a world with highly mobile investment capital comparative advantage is not enough. To attract capital, countries must have absolute advantages. That means they must be able to offer investors a better deal than any other country can. Unless a country has sufficient infrastructure, an educated and healthy work force, world-class managers and professionals and well-functioning institutions it probably won't be able to do so. The only thing likely to attract investment to countries that lack these conditions is the opportunity to rapidly exploit a small set of valuable natural resources, such as minerals, timber, prime agricultural land and exotic wildlife, that cannot easily be obtained elsewhere at low prices. To get beyond being targets of rent-seeking investments and ultimately to prosper over the long-term, countries have to focus on creating the conditions mentioned above and on managing their natural resources as sustainably as possible.

Experience from many regions around the world suggests that unless governments feel accountable to the wider society they are likely to pursue their private agendas and work for their personal material gain. Given that reality and the weak development of civil society and the private sector in southern Africa, it should come as no surprise that these countries have found it hard to develop democratic, transparent and efficient public institutions. It also implies that the only way to really improve the public institutions is to strengthen the region's non-governmental organizations, business associations, trade unions, representative local governments, farmer organizations, universities and mass media.

Control over valuable natural resources, and the rents they provide, make it particularly easy for governments not to feel accountable to other segments of society. Such rents allow governments to sustain their activities without having to negotiate with other groups about how high taxes will be and what they can expect to get in return from the government. Unless agencies that provide foreign assistance actively seek input from civil society, providing central government agencies with access to transfers of foreign assistance can have a similar effect.

Privatizing control over natural resources and other sources of government wealth is unlikely to solve the problem. One runs a strong risk of simply substituting public rent seeking with private rent seeking. That may be good for the foreign companies and powerful elites that get their hands on the resources. But unless the public closely scrutinizes the process, the deals that emerge are unlikely to benefit the poor.

Many of the people who work in international development agencies feel uncomfortable about acknowledging these stark realities. This book looks the problems straight in the eye. It carefully analyzes how the economic and political reforms in Tanzania, Zambia and Zimbabwe have affected the economic sectors based on natural resources such as agriculture, mining, tourism and forestry, and what that has meant for poor people and the environment. More importantly, it asks why the reform processes evolved in the way they did. What is it about the political economy of these situations that explains why some policies emerge and others do not? In other words, why have different groups within the international agencies and government bureaucracies supported particular policies and why have certain groups prevailed over others?

The author concludes that the recent transfer of control over natural resources in the three southern African countries mostly benefited foreign companies and the domestic elite. On some occasions small farmers and local communities also improved their access to natural resources on which their wellbeing depends. Institutional reforms such as land reform, decentralization and the creation of resource authorities have met with mixed results. In a few cases they have improved poor people's access to resources and the decision-making process. Certain recent reforms in Tanzania provide prominent examples of that. In many other situations, however, the reforms have fostered rampant corruption and monopolistic practices. None of the three countries has managed to develop effective institutions for regulating the negative environmental impacts of mining, farming or tourism.

This is not, however, a book about doom and gloom. It is a book about rediscovering the Zimbabwe I once knew. Despite all of the negative international trends, the people of southern Africa still have a chance to build societies that can make them proud. Returning to those dreams demands a view of development that goes well beyond a narrow set of short-term economic indicators. It requires bringing the hopes, beliefs, skills, culture and energy of southern Africa's people back to centre stage. As one glossy World Bank publication recently put it, we must start thinking about the *quality* of growth. Countries that currently have little to offer except for their labour and natural resources must protect and nurture those two vital resources in order to survive. Otherwise they will inevitably move from boom to bust. Building a strong civil society and a vibrant, efficient national business community is a central part of that process.

For international financial institutions to facilitate such an effort they will have to change a few key aspects of how they do business. Desk officers and task managers must have solid information about how their proposed policy reforms may affect poor people and the environment. They must stop seeing civil society as a nuisance they have to deal with and start viewing it as the backbone of long-term economic prosperity. They need stronger incentives, including both carrots and sticks, for adopting this broader vision of development. And, like everyone else concerned about southern Africa, they need to read this book

David Kaimowitz
Director General
Center for International Forestry Research
Bogor, Indonesia

Acknowledgements

This publication arises from the efforts of WWF's Macroeconomics Program Office (MPO) to work with national governments and international development agencies in increasing the attention given to environmental and equity concerns as the countries of southern Africa undergo economic reforms. Many colleagues have contributed to this effort over the past four years and to them I would like to extend my deepest appreciation for the support, guidance and patience.

First, I would like to acknowledge the commitment of policy makers and managers in seven development agencies in trying to strengthen the profile of environmental and social issues in structural reform programmes. Their support included providing financial resources, serving on the project's International Advisory Committee, organizing seminars within their respective agencies and undertaking various activities to share the conclusions with a broad audience. For these numerous contributions I would like to pay particular thanks to Amos Tincani, Artur Runge-Metzger, Simon LeGrand and Marina Kmentt of the European Commission, DG Development; Mats Segnestam, Dag Ehrenpreis, Tomas Andersson and Iftekhar Hossain of the Swedish International Development Agency; Erik Fiil, the late Jorgen Hartnack, and Torben Christensen of the Danish Ministry of Foreign Affairs (Danida); Soe Lin, John Summerbell, Sam Landon and Judi Allen from the Canadian International Development Agency; Eckehard Weiss, Ulrich Lutteken and Hans Martin Schmid of the Deutsche Gesellschaft fur Technische Zusammernarbeit (GTZ); Hans Peter Schipulle of the Bundesministerium fur Wirtschaftliche Zusammernarbeit und Entwicklung (BMZ);

Nadine Speich and Kathryn Imboden of the Swiss Development Cooperation. Their sustained involvement and support for the project does not imply institutional endorsement or agreement with the analysis and opinions offered in the essays constituting this publication.

The analytical and advocacy work on which this publication is based was carried out by local partners in the four countries of the region. The project in Tanzania was carried out at the Economics Research Bureau of the University of Dar es Salaam under the guidance of Kassim Kulindwa along with colleagues Oswald Mashindano, Hussein Sosovele and Fanuel Shechambo. Guy Scott and Charlotte Harland, joined by Gilbert Mudenda, Wynter Kabimba and Ivan Stubbs, conducted the research and advocacy programme in Zambia through Mano Consultancy, Ltd.. ZERO, Regional Environment Organization, implemented the programme in Zimbabwe under the guidance of Bheki Maboyi, Ramos Mabugu and Rabsan Dhlodhlo with contributions from Margaret Chitiga, Zivanai Tamangani, Emmanuel Guveya, Abby Mugugu and Augustine Masomera. The programme in South Africa was implemented through the Development Bank of Southern Africa under the coordination of Glynn Davies with support from Stephen Gelb, Barbara Schreiner and Saliem Fakir. In each country national advisory committees representing broad sectors of their respective societies provided guidance and support in many diverse and vital ways. I would like to extend my deep gratitude to all those who supported the project over the past four years as they worked under difficult conditions.

Staff from the World Bank provided steady contributions to the development of the project. Foremost, I would like to highlight the efforts of Jan Bojö that included attending international advisory committee meetings, commenting on draft reports, offering numerous suggestions and organizing several seminars with colleagues inside the World Bank. I would also like to thank his many colleagues who, likewise, offered comments and suggestions in the spirit of learning from and strengthening the studies of local partners with particular mention to: Albert Agbonyitor, Vandana Chandra, Robert Clement-Jones, Tekola Dejene, Peter Dewees, Anders Ekbom, Francois Falloux, Kirk Hamilton, Wendy Hughes, Imogene Jensen, Remi Kini, Gene Tidrick and Brigida Tuason. While the Bank staff sought to strengthen the outputs and contributions of the project, they bear no responsibility, collectively or individually, for the views presented in this work.

Colleagues in the WWF Network contributed in innumerable ways over the past four years to making this publication possible, including contributions from WWF's International Secretariat, WWF-Denmark, WWF-South Africa, WWF-Sweden, WWF-Switzerland and WWF-US. Among the many colleagues who supported this work I would like to thank Maria Boulos, Jenny Heap and Kevin Lyonette from the WWF International Secretariat, Tony Long, Herve Lefeuvre and Evelyne Rottiers of the European Policy Office, David Cumming, Ivan Bond and Monica Chundama from the Southern Africa Regional Programme Office, Paul Siegel of the Tanzania Programme Office and the members of the MPO Board. MPO staff in Washington, particularly Ainsley Foulds and Monica Chacon-Glenn, provided the daily administrative, contractual and financial reporting on which the project and final publication depended. To colleagues from WWF-US, Lee Zahnow, Addis Gizaw, Lisa Broadwell and Laura Bennett, I extend my gratitude for their support in administering this project with all the complexities of managing a project financed in five currencies. Brent Nordstrom, Maria Pia Iannariello, Pablo Gutman and Shubh Kumar-Range of the Macro-economics Program Office provided many comments and guidance over the past years to help the project through many challenges. I extend special thanks to Ola Larsson for his perseverance in serving as the project manager over the project's four-year duration.

I would like to express my appreciation to Pamela Stedman-Edwards and John D Shilling, acting as reviewers and critics, who helped turned early versions into the somewhat more polished essays of this final publication. Thanks to Doug and Steve Hellinger for their suggestions on the book's conclusions and recommendations.

The guidance and advice of these many friends and colleagues in no way diminishes the responsibility that I assume for the analysis and opinions offered herein. As interpretive essays, this publication does not represent formal policy of WWF but rather reflects the views of the author alone for which I assume full and final responsibility.

David Reed, PhD

Acronyms and Abbreviations

ADMADE	Administrative Management Design for Game Management Areas
BMZ	Bundesministerium für wirtschaftliche Zusammenarbeit und Entwicklung
BSAC	British South Africa Company
CAMPFIRE	Communal Areas Management Programme for Indigenous Resources (Zimbabwe)
CCM	Chama Cha Mapinduzi (Tanzania)
CIDA	Canadian International Development Agency
Danida	Danish International Development Agency
DBSA	Development Bank of Southern Africa
EIA	environmental impact assessment
ERB	Economics Research Bureau of the University of Dar es Salaam
ESAP	Economic and Social Adjustment Programme (Tanzania)/Economic Structural Adjustment Programme (Zimbabwe)
FEMATA	Federation of Miners' Associations of Tanzania
GDP	gross domestic product
GTZ	Deutsche Gesellschaft für Technische Zusammenarbeit
IMF	International Monetary Fund
INDECO	Industrial Development Corporation (Zambia)
LSCF	large-scale commercial farms
MMD	Movement for Multiparty Democracy (Zambia)

NAMBOARD	National Agricultural Marketing Board (Zambia)
NGO	non-governmental organization
NLP	National Land Policy (Tanzania)
SDC	Swiss Development Corporation
Sida	Swedish International Development Agency
STAMICO	State Mining Corporation (Tanzania)
TANU	Tanganyika African National Union
TTC	Tanzania Tourist Corporation
UDI	Unilateral Declaration of Independence (Southern Rhodesia)
UN	United Nations
UNIP	United National Independence Party (Zambia)
URT	United Republic of Tanzania
WWF	World Wide Fund for Nature
WWF	World Wildlife Fund (United States and Canada)
ZANU-PF	Zimbabwe African National Union Patriotic Front
ZAPU	Zimbabwe African People's Union
ZAWA	Zambian Wildlife Authority
ZCCM	Zambian Consolidated Copper Mines
ZIMCO	Zambian Industrial and Mining Corporation
ZIMPREST	Zimbabwe Programme for Economic and Social Transformation

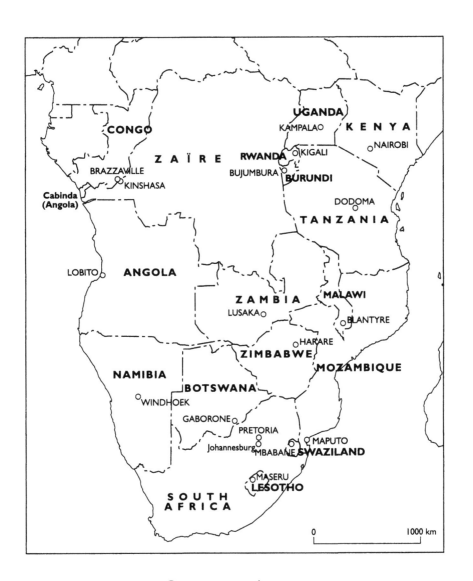

SOUTHERN AFRICA

Introduction

Natural resource wealth has been both a blessing and a curse for countries on the African continent for the better part of five centuries. Natural resources provided the economic foundation on which great African kingdoms were erected as, in equal measure, they generated the income on which the major European colonial empires were built. At times, salt, gold and diamonds served as the catalyst for wealth accumulation for nobility; in other periods, copper, cobalt and cocoa generated financial returns from which multinational corporations acquired their global reach.

Given the centuries-long dynamic of conflict, competition and conquest associated with natural resource wealth in Africa, it is hardly surprising that natural resources should remain central to the economic reforms implemented in all African countries during the last two decades of the 20th century and into the new millennium. As intended, those countries' economic reform programmes – whether home-grown or supported by the World Bank and other development agencies – have had significant impacts on natural resources through, for instance, restructuring mining and tourism sectors and through changes in the ways that rural communities use forests, wildlife, water and land. While designed to bring about changes in the role of natural resources in the countries' development process, the ultimate outcomes of the adjustment process were frequently quite different from the original goals of the designers. Frequently the rural poor, allegedly the intended beneficiaries of the reforms, were the social group most heavily burdened by the economic changes.

This book presents a series of essays which examine the role that natural resources have played in creating economic structures and systems of governance in three African countries: Tanzania, Zambia and Zimbabwe. They also discuss the ways in which the resulting political regimes have exerted strong influence over efforts to restructure those economies. By analysing the relation between natural resources, statist economic systems and authoritarian political regimes, these essays seek to bring into focus specific challenges that these countries must address in order to promote more equitable, democratic societies pursing sustainable development strategies.

It is fair to ask from the outset, however: Why another set of essays on economic change in sub-Saharan Africa? Have not these issues been examined by hundreds of analysts from the World Bank, academia and government agencies over the past years? Have not all the basic issues been settled, and generally accepted answers been provided after such debate? Unquestionably, the great wealth of material on these topics produced in the 1980s and early 1990s provided a wide range of interpretations and new understandings of the dynamics of economic reform.

Consider, however, the following. The essays in this book arise from a different perspective. They grow from the efforts of groups from civil society to address the environmental and social dimensions of economic reforms. They emanate from the costs of adjustment policies that have accumulated over the past 20 years, costs that have fallen disproportionately on the poor and politically marginal groups of these societies, and which are being transmitted to society at large through environmental degradation and social imbalances. They arise from the imperative to become more effective in addressing the social and environmental dimensions of the economic reforms still being implemented in these societies.

The debate about the impact of adjustment on the societies of sub-Saharan Africa over recent years identified many important issues, led to the development of numerous analytical perspectives, and identified various options and paths for future policy makers. But civil society – that is, the amalgam of groups and movements that has emerged in response to the social and environmental shortcomings of the growth enterprise – must now, 20 years later, respond to the growing costs that have fallen on society at large. From WWF's point of view, the previous debate among policy makers holds many lessons from which we have much to learn. However, we must continue analysing the problems besetting societies from our distinct viewpoint as an international environmental organization. Likewise we must seek answers to environmental concerns that are not necessarily those articulated by government policy makers or international development agencies. This series of essays, then, is an initial analysis that should form the basis for articulating and promoting more effective policies and institutional arrangements. Ultimately we hope to promote more sustainable, equitable development paths and more responsive institutions that operate on the logic of sustainability, not just short-term growth.

ORIGINS

The origins of this publication lie in analytical work that WWF carried out during the 1990s to document the impact of structural adjustment on the environment in developing and transition countries.[1] From that analysis we recognized that the environmental effects of structural reforms are transmitted through two distinct, yet complementary, paths. The first path, the direct effects, result from changing relative prices in an economy through changes in monetary, fiscal, exchange rate and trade policy, among other factors. Such direct effects included, for example, price changes that affect water, energy, fertilizers and other inputs in production processes, thereby changing the intensity of resource use and levels of environmental externalities. Changing exchange rate policies, another example, affect the price of goods traded across borders and, with new market opportunities, encourage new production patterns that often result in impacts on natural resources and the environment. These effects have both positive and negative environmental effects depending, in large measure, on the existing price and incentive structures.

The second path, the indirect effects, tends to be more difficult to track despite the fact that it is far more pervasive and often enduring. These indirect effects are expressed primarily through two mechanisms.

Foremost, changes in the labour markets and social classes – that is, the way that people earn their living – generate widespread and enduring environmental impacts. The most significant of these impacts is the downward pressure on the incomes of the rural poor who, in consequence, intensify pressures on the natural resources on which their livelihoods depend. The second principal mechanism by which these indirect effects are transmitted to the environment is through changes in institutional arrangements that change the ability of governments to establish and maintain environmental management regimes. Some countries experience reductions in government spending for the environmental patrimony. Other countries embark on institutional reforms that change land tenure and resource management authorities. Invariably these changes influence the ways in which economic agents and social groups interact with the country's natural resource base.

The conclusions drawn from 12 country case studies led WWF to formulate a series of recommendations to change policies of national governments and international development agencies so as to better address the environmental dimension of economic reforms. Foremost among those recommendations were the following:

- Put in place transition strategies by which the rural poor can adjust to the new economic conditions and incentive structures resulting from economic reforms. These transition strategies seek to ensure that the rural poor do not suffer irreparable damage to their income-earning capacity as a result of the structural reforms. These strategies were intended, in turn, to reduce the pressure on the rural poor that leads to their drawing down natural capital to survive.
- Develop a strategic vision of the role of natural resources and environmental goods and services in the economic transformation of extractive and agricultural economies into more diversified, complex economic structures. That strategic environmental vision should guide public investment and shape the evolution of national institutions so as to ensure the sustainability of the emerging economy.
- Apply environmental impact assessments (EIAs) for all structural adjustment lending operations. Above all, such assessments were intended to establish monitoring systems at the national level by

which stakeholders and the concerned public could hold both government and development agencies accountable for the environmental outcomes of structural reforms.

The conclusions and recommendations were received with studied scepticism by the Bretton Woods institutions, still unwilling to accept (at the time of publication in 1992 and 1996) anything but a narrow interpretation of the environmental impacts of the reform programmes.[2]

FROM ANALYSIS TO ADVOCACY

In contrast to the scepticism of the World Bank and IMF, other multilateral and bilateral development agencies accepted WWF's conclusions more willingly, primarily because the analysis confirmed their own institutional experiences in a wide range of developing and transition countries.[3] Above all, the studies brought into focus the complex interactions between economic reforms, growing poverty and accompanying environmental impacts. These development agencies felt that a concerted effort should be undertaken to support the implementation of a number of specific recommendations derived from the analytical work. Their support grew from their own institutional mandates to help put the countries on more sustainable development paths from which long-term income improvements and sustainable resource use could flow.

As agreed with the seven development agencies, an advocacy and capacity-building project was designed consisting of four distinct yet complementary activities over a three-year period in four African countries, as follows.

- Analysis: Local partners would analyse the dynamics of at least one natural resource sector, attempting to understand how economic reforms in the chosen sector were affecting the environment.
- Policy formulation: Local partners would identify specific measures that government, the private sector and civil society could undertake to address the most serious environmental problems developing in the various sectors.

- Capacity building and training: Together with WWF, local partners would provide a range of training, public education and capacity-building activities for specific groups of stakeholders.
- Advocacy: Local partners would undertake those measures required to mitigate, complement or fundamentally change the economic reform process to strengthen environmental and economic outcomes.

WWF's local partners in the four countries ranged from NGOs to private firms to parastatal financial institutions. In South Africa, the Development Bank of Southern Africa served as the local project executant. In Tanzania, the Economics Research Bureau (ERB) of the University of Dar es Salaam organized and implemented the project. In Zambia a private consulting firm, MANO, served as the project coordinator while ZERO, a regional environmental organization, assumed project responsibilities in Zimbabwe.

The four project partners carried out research into specific natural resource sectors selected because of their centrality to the countries' economies and the economic reform process. For example, Tanzania focused on the mining and tourism sectors, Zimbabwe on tourism and Zambia on rural livelihoods, while South Africa focused on water and energy pricing regimes. Following the initial research activities, measures were identified to strengthen the impact of the specific reforms on both economic performance and environmental sustainability.[4] In addition, each local partner carried out a wide range of training and advocacy activities designed to increase public understanding and deliver recommendations to appropriate policy makers in the respective countries. These activities included the following examples.

- The ERB in Tanzania developed documentary programmes for public dissemination consisting of 39 15-minute radio episodes and 11 30-minute video episodes for a television documentary on the social and environmental impacts of mining and tourism.
- ZERO provided training events for private sector and government officials on tourism and the environment in Zimbabwe.

- MANO organized a permanent forum in Lusaka, the national capital, to represent rural communities engaged in land disputes in Zambia.
- The Development Bank of Southern Africa held briefings and published articles to promote pricing policy reforms in water and energy in South Africa.

A Broadened Perspective

The research and advocacy experiences in the four countries raised a series of questions that economic analysis could not adequately explain. Foremost among those challenges was trying to understand the political mechanisms by which groups from civil society could influence decision-making processes and ultimately ensure that environmental concerns were addressed in national economic and social policy. That concern arose directly from the seemingly impenetrable political barriers that confronted partners as they tried to promote policy recommendations in Tanzania, Zambia and Zimbabwe. While mechanisms of electoral democracy had been established in Tanzania, Zambia and Zimbabwe those electoral processes often seemed designed to shroud autocratic rule and assuage international opinion rather than to create accessible mechanisms of public accountability and transparency.

What our partners confronted were political systems in which political and economic elite groups used their access to government bureaucracy to promote policies that benefited a very limited number of individuals and privileged groups. Decades of authoritarian rule in those countries had limited the means and opportunities by which the concerned public and stakeholders could influence prevailing policy and institutional arrangements. Moreover, institutions had been organized by autocratic regimes to exclude and marginalize many groups and social sectors of those societies.

Trying to influence the design and implementation of economic reforms, particularly those supported by the Bretton Woods institutions, is a daunting challenge even under the best political conditions. As we came to realize during the advocacy activities associated with this project, the World Bank and IMF also faced challenges as they tried to shape the economic policies of these resource-based economies. However, for groups of civil society in countries without a strong tradition of public advocacy and still living in the shadow of authoritarianism, promoting policy changes that touched the natural resource sectors proved virtually impossible.

The five essays comprising this publication are the result of our efforts to understand the complex dynamics that operate between statist economies, forms of governance and natural resource wealth. They also offer interpretations of the impact that structural reform programmes have had on those complex, often conflictual, dynamics. The first essay highlights the role that natural resources have played as newly independent countries organized their economic systems and established national political regimes. This essay underscores the different problems that natural resource wealth creates in establishing mechanisms of public accountability and sound economic management.

The subsequent three chapters highlight the experiences in the countries covered in this project: Tanzania, Zambia and Zimbabwe.[5] The aim of each is to understand how the economic structures inherited from the colonial experience were reshaped during the decades following independence as new leaders constructed statist economies based on natural resource wealth. That historical background provides a framework for interpreting the difficulties and challenges experienced as economic reform programmes tried to privatize the economies and open them to international markets. We focus, above all, on the impacts on the rural poor and the opportunities, or loss of them, associated with the economic restructuring process.

The final chapter offers a series of more general conclusions about the outcomes of economic reforms in these resource-based economies. These conclusions focus on the ways that the rural poor have lost control over natural resource wealth and have been marginalized by institutional reforms that are a result of the adjustment process. We also offer several recommendations to address those problems.

The Analytical Approach

In moving beyond a strict economic rationality, we have used a political economy perspective to decipher the complex interactions among the economic, political and social actors involved in the process of change. By political economy we mean the dynamic interaction between social groups, economic agents and states as they pursue wealth and power in national and international arenas. In using this concept, several points warrant clarification. A political economy approach requires that we try to understand the actions and impacts not only of individual actors but also of social groups and the state as they compete with one another in pursuit of wealth and power. It means looking across social arenas – that is, into the political, sociological and cultural, as well as the economic, fields in which these different actors operate in order to understand the outcomes associated with changing economic structures. This approach also obliges us to consider the interaction among actors on the national level as well as those working on the international stage.

Finally, it is important to point out that there is no one correct or universally applicable approach for understanding the dynamics of development. In some cases economic analysis must be given greater emphasis to decipher societal change. In certain circumstances, econometrics and modelling can provide important insights into behaviour and outcomes. In other cases, political or sociological analysis is best able to explain how actors have influenced the developmental process. Institutional analysis, political mapping, game theory and other approaches may be the most useful tools in such circumstances. In short, a good analytical approach is one that is able to identify the essential factors or forces that drive change. Moreover, a good analytical approach, by presenting a sharp summary of causalities, should facilitate the identification of the means and measures to be employed to move social behaviour in a desired direction – in this case, to improve the environmental performance of countries as they undertake economic reforms.

In consideration of the various analytical approaches, we felt that a political economy approach was best able to explain the complex dynamics in each country and the region. It helped us understand the behaviour of political actors and the institutional contexts in which they operated, the influence of economic policies and incentives, the functioning of the state, and the central role of natural resource wealth. Moreover, we felt that a political economy approach could best decipher the dynamics among actors at the local, national, and international levels, dynamics that are not susceptible to quantitative analysis and interpretation.

Limitations

As with any research methodology, this approach embodies its own set of limitations that the reader must bear in mind in assessing the merits of the essays that follow. For example, when considering the dynamics between natural resource wealth, political systems and economic structures over an extended period of time, we are obliged to operate at a rather high level of generality. As a consequence, many important events, influential actors, and societal experiences are compressed, perhaps distorted, in assessing outcomes and processes of change. Moreover, the incompleteness of the economic reform process currently underway in the three countries invariably introduces many uncertainties and unknowns.

For these reasons, we do not pretend to present all-inclusive analyses or offer a final balance sheet of winners and losers, costs and benefits. The purpose of the essays is to identify a series of societal processes and changes that are taking place and to raise what seem to be central issues for policy makers in the countries and international development agencies. It is our hope that careful identification of these challenges will encourage broader discussion and, thereafter, policy responses to address these concerns. Above all, we hope that the work will contribute in some modest way to strengthening the abilities of groups from civil society to respond to the many challenges posed by natural resource wealth to their goals of promoting equitable, democratic societies.

David Reed
Washington
June 2001

Chapter 1

The Political Economy of
Natural Resource Wealth

The essential concern of this work is the relationship between macro-economic change and the resource patrimony of three countries of southern Africa. Regarding the first part of our concern, macroeconomic reforms, no region of the world has generated more controversy, more analysis or more publications than has the economic reform experience of sub-Saharan Africa. The protracted duration of stabilization and adjustment programmes in the region, the disappointing outcomes, the persistence of poverty, faltering privatization initiatives, continuing fiscal deficits, lack of foreign direct investment, and a host of themes too innumerable to inventory have preoccupied African rulers and the international development community for two decades. And with good reason. Now, as two decades ago, the region continues to experience economic difficulties and setbacks unlike any other, despite the continuing commitment to implement adjustment programmes in pursuit of ever-illusive macroeconomic stability.

The second part of our concern, the countries' natural resource patrimony, has seldom been directly addressed by policy makers. The main approach followed by the World Bank and other lending agencies has been through sectoral policies seeking to increase productivity, opening the sectors to foreign investors, and deepening ties to global markets. As a result, the full impact of natural resource wealth on economies, systems of governance and social relations has largely been ignored.

In contrast to that segmented approach, we believe that natural resources are central to the difficulty in reforming the economies of many countries of the region. The appropriation of natural resource rents and mismanagement of natural resource wealth have provided the foundation of statist economies and authoritarian political regimes from which countries of the region have yet to thoroughly extract themselves.

In this first essay we focus on the ways that economic structures and systems of governance are tied directly to the countries' natural resources. In the first section of this chapter we review the dynamics by which colonial powers constructed economic relations dependent on, and explicitly limited to, extraction of natural resource wealth in Africa. Following this historical overview we discuss how the resource-based economies of the newly independent states lent themselves to statist economic regimes and authoritarian political systems that became entrenched in subsequent decades. The third section of the essay examines the ways that structural reforms intersected with statist economies, often generating results not anticipated by designers and managers of the reform process. To close, we highlight a number of specific challenges associated with natural resources, including declining terms of trade and corruption, that continue to plague economies of the region.

We hope that this general background, one that is often skirted because of its sensitive political nature, will shed light on many of the challenges encountered as economic reforms were implemented in the 1980s and 1990s and on the distribution of benefits and losses as societies underwent structural change. In turn, we hope it will sharpen understanding of the role that systems of governance, notably those marked by authoritarianism, play in determining how natural resources are (mis)used in the development process of resource-based economies.

Natural Resource Wealth

The Scramble for Africa

While so near from a geographic point of view, European powers largely ignored the African continent for more than three centuries as Portuguese, British and Dutch merchants sought spices, precious metals, and then markets for manufactured goods in Asia and Latin America. During the 15th and 16th centuries, European traders established commercial ties as they searched for gold along coastal and riverain areas of West Africa. Those commercial ties remained, however, relatively anecdotal from the colonial powers' point of view when compared to investments and national prestige committed to pursuing the spice trade in the East Indies, developing gold and silver mines in Potosi, Huancavelica and Mexico, and extracting agricultural taxes in India (Booth et al 1990, Wolpert 1989). European interest in Africa increased at the close of the 17th century when traders supplanted their search for gold and diamonds with purchase of slaves to be sold to the aristocracy in Europe and, more importantly, to plantation owners in the New World. It was, as Walter Rodney points out, the slave trade that 'led to commercial domination of Africa by Europe' from which African economies would fail to break their dependence in subsequent centuries (Rodney 1982). As the European economy expanded and diversified in the 18th and 19th centuries, and as moral objections to slavery increased in Europe and North America, the returns from slave raids diminished relative to the financial returns generated by using coerced labour to produce and export agricultural goods to European capitals and to extract raw materials for European industry (Oliver and Atmore 1967).

Fundamental change in European investment in Africa did not come until the mid-1800s, when European monarchs and ministers became convinced that geopolitical preeminence on the European continent depended on the breadth of colonial dominions, notably those in the African continent. Earlier commercial ties allowed the French, Portuguese and British to establish colonial claims that crisscrossed the continent, although effective colonial control remained limited to coastal areas. Fearing that he would be relegated to the status of a petty monarch in the European theatre, King Leopold II of Belgium sought desperately to build his own empire in the heart of the 'Dark Continent'. The 1876 report of young explorer Verney Cameron, the first white explorer to cross southern Africa, proclaiming 'the interior [of Africa] is mostly a magnificent and healthy country of unspeakable richness', further intensified Leopold's obsession with making Belgium a colonial power. Leopold II set the stage for his diplomatic moves by convening the Geological Conference in Brussels later that same year (Pakenham 1991; Hochschild 1999).

Fulfilment of his colonial aspirations, however, was placed on hold until the Conference of Berlin of 1884 when Prince Bismarck, the ruler of the second Reich, brought together 14 greater and lesser nations to agree on the terms by which established and aspiring colonial powers were to control the largely unexplored African continent (Pakenham 1991). The conference was, in many ways, the culmination of a decade of conflict and competition among those nations as they sought to establish political jurisdiction over the peoples and resources of the continent. At the same time, however, the two-and-a-half-month-long conference represented a new stage in that international rivalry as European nations sought to extend the new balance of power on the continent to rights and privileges in dominating the African continent.

From that cauldron of diplomatic intrigue, Leopold II emerged as the principal beneficiary as he gained control of the greatest source of natural resource wealth in the very centre of the continent, the Congo basin. For his part, Bismarck carved out space for German colonies in Cameroon, Togoland, South West Africa and German East Africa, while checking France, Portugal and Britain's efforts to expand their already considerable colonial domains. For the ensuing 30 years, the colonial powers were able to exploit Africa's natural wealth and human labour with impunity until the European rulers' ambition caused the continent to be engulfed by the Great War (First World War) of 1914–18 (Wesseling 1997; Collins 1996).

Initial Returns

The immediate motivation driving what historians have termed 'the scramble for Africa' was the conviction held by European policy makers that colonial expansion was the key to emerging from the economic depression (1873–96) besetting the industrializing economies of Europe and North America. While political leaders hoped for quick returns from the colonial enterprise, the long economic contraction precluded substantial investments in the colonies' infrastructure and similarly dampened commercial ventures during the last part of the 19th century. Financial returns to the European powers remained quite meagre for the remainder of the century, and it was not until the beginning of the 20th century that the colonial system experienced a 15-year period of steady economic growth generating returns which began to match initial expectations.

During the period between 1900 and the beginning of the First World War, economic imperatives dominated colonial policy. This period witnessed a dramatic increase in global trade as colonies experienced unprecedented annual growth rates such as 29.4 per cent in the Gold Coast and 26.4 per cent in Nigeria (Havinden and Meredith 1993). Uganda, Kenya, Southern Rhodesia (Zimbabwe) and Northern Rhodesia (Zambia) in eastern Africa experienced similar growth in tradables during this period. The pattern of trade between Europe and the African colonies was 'a classical one of exports of raw materials and foods and imports of a wide range of manufactured goods and fuels. Without any industries of their own, the tropical colonies remained a buoyant market for the industrial exports of Britain and Europe' (Havinden and Meredith 1993). Demand for raw materials and foodstuffs from Africa continued to grow as industrialization and urbanization accelerated in Europe. At the same time, manufactured items from the European industrial centres were both cheap and abundant as African populations sought the material benefits associated with burgeoning international commerce.

Private enterprise invested substantially in profitable production and extractive industries. During this period many of the great food processing, mining and banking companies established their economic foundations on the African continent from which global empires were later to emerge. Among the most notable was Lever Brothers, later to become Unilever, which built its edible oils empire on the palm oil plantations of Nigeria and Congo. Firestone established its rubber plantations in Liberia during this period. Cadbury Brothers deepened their commercial investments in the cocoa plantations of West Africa. Other companies established their overseas investments in Africa during the first decade of the century from which fortunes in tea, sisal, copper, gold, diamonds, cocoa, coffee, bananas and cotton, among others, were made (Rodney 1982). To support the growing commerce, colonial administrations offered ample subsidies to private investors, organized systems of governance of local populations, imposed head and hut taxes to finance local administrations, and provided the military apparatus to guarantee stability in the colonial realms (Wesseling 1997). However, during this period of rapidly expanding trade, private enterprise adamantly refused to invest in the infrastructure required to extract the raw materials from the hinterland of the African colonies. Hence, to fulfill their policy objectives, the colonial powers found themselves obliged to finance a growing list of infrastructure projects primarily for the construction of railroads, harbours and, later, highways on which private enterprise could flourish.

Buttressing the economic imperatives, geopolitical motives also shaped colonial policy as European powers constantly sought to fend off encroachments by competitors. This political manoeuvring had particular significance for East Africa. The British East Africa Protectorate in the 1890s seemed particularly vulnerable to incursions from German colonial investments in Tanganyika lying to the south and French advances from the French Congo to the west. In order to establish its firm control in East Africa, Britain declared Uganda and Kenya separate colonies after the turn of the century and quickly set about erecting formal colonial administrations and initiating economic activities to attract private investors. Securing these colonies was an integral part of Great Britain's geopolitical aspirations of controlling eastern Africa from Cairo to Cape Town, thereby protecting strategic access to India through the Suez Canal and the Cape of Good Hope (Davis and Huttenback 1986).

The World Wars and Between

The economies of most African colonies remained comparatively unaffected by the tumultuous events on the continent as the colonial powers waged the First World War. The most immediate effect of the war on the natural resource wealth of Africa was to stimulate demand in strategic commodities, for instance for copper, rubber, sisal and cotton. Concomitantly, the war years depressed demand for cocoa, coffee, tea, fruit and other commodities not required by the war effort. Overall, the war ushered in a period of declining terms of trade for raw materials and commodities that had experienced a slow but steady rise in previous decades (Brett 1973).

The terms of peace at the Paris Peace Conference of 1918 realigned control of overseas territories around the world, but nowhere as significantly as in Africa. For example, Germany was virtually removed from the continent as its colonies in Africa were divided among the French and British. The French acquired vital areas of West Africa including Cameroon, while the British were granted control of German West African colonies, thereby allowing Britain to move closer to fulfilling its aspiration of extending British control from Cairo to Cape Town (Oliver and Atmore 1967).

The accumulated war debts of the European powers and the continuing high rates of unemployment dictated important changes in colonial relations (Brett 1973). Those two domestic concerns drove the British Colonial Office, for example, to implement policies that would generate considerably higher yields for the motherland through a more 'comprehensive programme of colonial development'. That programme included increasing investment in the colonies' infrastructure so as to increase export of British steel, create employment, increase the flow of commodities for processing in the homeland, and expand export of manufactured goods. The results of that policy for the British Empire and its colonies, particularly for eastern and southern Africa, warrant attention:

The twin pillars of British colonial economic policy were reinforced during the 1920s. Private enterprise remained predominantly British and the rise of native capitalism was resisted. The
colonial economies remained complementary to the British
economy, providing foodstuffs, raw materials and absorbing
manufactured goods. The degree of dependence on a narrow
range of primary exports increased in most cases, and tendencies
towards the colonial economies becoming less complementary
were successfully resisted. The general economic experience of
the colonies under British rule from 1900 to 1929 was one of
bursts of growth in the export sector, but not development
towards the creation of a strong diversified economy which
might be regarded as a more appropriate fulfillment of 'trusteeship' (Havinden and Meredith 1993).

Colonial Africa struggled through the Depression of the 1930s in the
face of falling demand for commodities, declining commodity prices,
and rising debt burdens of colonial administrations. Perhaps no region
was hit as hard as East Africa, which had recently contracted significant
debt liabilities to London to finance infrastructure expansion, often
designed to stimulate demand for British industry and services. Falling
coffee, tea, sisal and cotton prices increased pressure on the colonies
which, in turn, passed financial hardship on to workers through lower
wages and to the populace more generally through increased hut taxes.
The quality of food, clothing and merchandise imports fell as local
populations could no longer afford higher quality goods from European
countries. That frequent uprisings, strikes and rioting should break out
and that anti-colonial sentiment should rise throughout the colonial
world, including in Africa, was not in the least surprising as the global
economic contraction continued for the better part of the decade (Oliver
and Atmore 1967).

As during the First World War, demand for commodities and raw
materials fell during the Second World War (1939–45) except for strategic minerals needed to produce military materiel. Likewise, shortages
of inputs, machinery and replacement parts were frequent as companies
diverted industrial output to support the war effort. Moreover, colonies

were obliged by their colonial masters to provide soldiers and workers for deployment in battles and factories thousands of miles from their African homes. Overall, investment, personnel and material support for colonial administrations fell dramatically during the war, leaving development imperatives for later years (Louis 1977).

Towards Decolonization

The six years following the Second World War brought the most dynamic growth period for the colonial world, including for the countries of eastern and southern Africa. Reconstruction of war-torn Europe spawned global demand for raw materials and foodstuffs, leading to an unprecedented rise in export values and trade volume for the colonial world. The period witnessed a steady rise in investment as international investors sought to expand access to raw materials, diversify sources of commodities, and stimulate demand for manufactured and capital goods.

The expansion of commodity production, coupled with the increasing investments from foreign companies, intensified the competition between colonial powers and the colonies. New opportunities arose in the colonies for processing commodities and minerals, expanding infrastructure and social services, and developing transportation and communications systems. Yet, while allowing expansion of infrastructure and services, often funded by long-term loans from European governments, the colonial powers resisted any form of industrial development that might compete with homeland manufacturers. Their primary policy focus was to ensure that colonies remained producers of raw materials and foodstuffs as inputs for European manufactured or processed goods. However, as many of the larger commodity producers in the colonies were overseas operations of British, French, Dutch, Belgian and Portuguese companies, the increased conflicts in the colonies involved not only Africans but Europeans as well (Havinden and Meredith 1993).

Ultimately, such conflicts between colonial policies and the developmental needs of the colonized gave rise to the struggles for national liberation waged during the 20 years following the Second World War. The process of decolonization opened with the independence of the Philippines and Indonesia in 1946, followed quickly by India and Pakistan in 1947. However, it was not until 1960, when 17 African countries acquired political independence, that decolonization altered the political dynamics across the continent (Comeliau 1991).

ECONOMIC FOUNDATIONS OF AUTHORITARIANISM

While the struggle for independence varied widely from country to country, African countries shared many characteristics that strongly marked the post-independence period. Foremost among them was economic dependence on natural resource wealth. The historical sketch presented above has highlighted the policy of European powers to limit the economic structures of African colonies to commodity production and raw material extraction and to resist efforts that might engender economic diversification and industrialization. As a result, African economies were fairly simple structures dependent on the export of a handful of commodities oriented to European, North American and Asian markets. The export orientation also rendered the economies highly vulnerable to global market fluctuations and climatic changes.

Following from the above, a second common feature of many African economies was the lack of dynamic entrepreneurial classes that could respond quickly to the removal of colonial era political and economic constraints and drive the economic diversification of the fledgling nations. At the time of independence, the economies of many countries relied heavily on the contribution of foreign mining and agricultural companies. The agricultural output of small-scale farmers producing for domestic consumption and, to a lesser degree, external markets, provided the second economic leg on which the new countries depended. There were very few African nationals who owned enterprises capable of competing in international markets. Their lack of capital, market access and technological capacity, among other factors, rendered nascent businesses highly vulnerable to international competition. In equal measure, there were few trade associations through which information and experience could be exchanged, economic policies could be formulated and proposed to government, or relations with other economic sectors could be developed. Finally, the legal and institutional infrastructure inherited from the colonial period created obstacles to market development in most countries. In short, the newly independent countries lacked the entrepreneurial foundations needed to drive economic development.

In this vacuum the new political elites, usually African leaders who had led independence struggles, assigned primary responsibility for charting and leading the growth process of the state. In the absence of dynamic entrepreneurial classes, African political leaders, where necessary, formed alliances with European companies which stayed in the country following independence, hoping to maintain the meagre economic foundations during the period of transition. In this context of change and vulnerability, it is hardly surprising that four principal forms of wealth accumulation dominated economic structures in the region: rent-seeking state capitalism, monopolistic production regimes, state regulation of smallholder commodity production, and plantation agriculture, each considered below (Bangura 1992; Ghai 1991).

Rent-seeking State Capitalism

With the state at the centre of economic development, rent-seeking state capitalism became the principal form of capital accumulation in the mining, agriculture and energy sectors. By expanding state control into natural resource sectors, governments ensured a steady flow of revenues with which to finance developmental priorities.

Monopoly Production

Along with pervasive rent seeking, monopoly production involving both parastatals and national and foreign companies dominated other economic sectors, production lines and markets. Often invoking the need to protect infant industries from external competition, national governments allowed private and parastatal monopolies to determine prices and market dynamics in a wide range of sectors including tourism, energy and transport.

Smallholder Commodity Production

The commanding position assumed by the state in economic affairs shaped the economic activities and opportunities of small and medium farmers. In essence, the state, by setting prices, controlling marketing systems, regulating the flow of information and organizing credit-making mechanisms, determined the terms and manner by which small and medium farms were linked to national and international markets. The potential dynamism and independence of small farmers and entrepreneurs were stifled by the dominant economic forces of monopoly and rent seeking which controlled the smallholder economy. Moreover, the control of small and medium commodity producers allowed governments to channel rents from the agricultural sector to subsidize urban workers as part of import-substitution industrialization strategies (Bangura and Gibbon 1992).

Large-scale Commercial Agriculture

One economic sector that escaped the control of state-driven economies was large-scale or plantation agriculture. Inherited from the colonial period, this sector was tied directly to international markets, both for inputs and market outlets, and was characterized by an economic responsiveness and dynamism unlike other sectors in the post-colonial economy. While the political elite made concerted efforts to bring this sector under state control, the economic strength and political independence of the large-scale producers prevented them from falling entirely under the control of the state apparatus (Mosley 1983; Skälnes 1995).

The state served as the locus of economic planning, manager of economic units and arbiter of all economic and political conflicts that arose as economic and social conditions changed. The state, moreover, became the repository of rents and revenues whose ultimate use was determined by a political elite acting in the name of the national good and public welfare. Under such conditions, ruling groups felt little need to create transparent political processes by which conflicts among competing economic and social groups could be resolved. Such conflicts, which are necessary companions of any economic growth process, were resolved through processes internal to the ruling party or elite group. Those internal decision-making processes determined how rents and revenues were distributed to individuals and to subgroups both within the elite group and in society at large. Without public accountability, graft and corruption became entrenched mechanisms used by rulers who decided how resource rents were to be distributed for private or public benefit.

AUTHORITARIAN REGIMES IN SOUTHERN AFRICA

The lack of an entrepreneurial class capable of driving the wealth accumulation process may explain why new political leaders of the post-independence period placed the state at the centre of the development enterprise. By the same token, however, we have to ask if the authoritarian regimes that sprang quickly out of the colonial period necessarily had to accompany the state-driven economic system. For, indeed, the ultimate paradox of the post-colonial period is that the new leaders relied on authoritarian rule, often degenerating into physical oppression and coercion, to pursue the nationalist goals for which the people had struggled for decades.

Few informed observers would hold that there was an automatic or deterministic relation between a statist economic system, natural resource wealth and the political authoritarianism endemic to sub-Saharan Africa. However, the prevailing development strategy of promoting 'accumulation from above' wherein the state drove the centralized accumulation process, owned and managed the nation's enterprises, and had the right to distribute wealth according to its own criteria, lent itself to centralized political control. Moreover, the comparative ease with which natural resources could be controlled and managed (though not necessarily profitably) by state corporations, further strengthened the impetus to place the state in charge of environmental assets of all kinds, ranging from forests, water, minerals, nature reserves and biodiversity, to the land itself (Ghai 1991; Sandbrook 1985).

With most productive assets and economic decision making centralized under state control, there was little hesitation to extend control of
the political elite to the social life of the emerging nations as well. A
critical factor in maintaining this centralized economic regime and
authoritarian political arrangement was ensuring the fealty of urban and
rural masses in whose name the rulers claimed to act. Although the
mobilized rural populations played a determinant role in anti-colonial
struggles, the rural citizenry remained outside the new political arrangements for all intents and purposes. At best, they were called into political
action when broad public pressure was needed to implement nationalist
policies vis-à-vis previous colonial powers, or when ruling parties needed
to generate mass support during elections or for specific policies
(Bangura 1992).

Analysts, however, do highlight the particularities of conditions in
the African post-colonial period that explain the consistency with which
authoritarianism arose in new countries and the tenacity with which it
has held sway over the past four decades (Nelson 1989; Bangura 1992;
Toye 1991; Mosley et al 1991; Gibbon 1995b; Skälnes 1995; Mpuku
and Zyuulu 1997). Included in those factors are:

- the weakness of political leaders and the narrowness of their political
  base located in urban areas or trade union movements;
- the difficulties in sustaining the involvement of rural populations in
  the society-wide transformations taking place;
- the distorted, weak institutional scaffolding inherited from the
  colonial regime;
- the requirements of defending the new nations from neocolonial
  pressures and intrigues of the imperial powers; and
- Cold War competition that obliged countries to opt between ideological camps.

The exact characterization of the authoritarian regimes that dominated
political and social life in the countries varies according to the country
and the specific time period under consideration. In the more benign
expression, regimes in the post-colonial period took the form of welfarism that bound the political authorities to the populace, albeit largely

urban populaces, in the form of a social contract (Gibbon 1992). That social contract endowed the new political elites with the authority to manage the economy, to control and regulate economic agents, and to generate national wealth so long as the public received the benefits of wealth accumulation through construction of infrastructure and welfare support, again for largely urban populations. This form of welfarism provided the rationale for the state's capture of resource rents from natural resource sectors and the peasantry. It also served as the public ideology for pursuing import-substitution industrialization attempted by countries included in this study.

Harsher, more repressive *dirigiste* regimes also characterized the political life of these countries at various times, particularly during periods of economic crisis and political instability. This *dirigiste* dynamic relied on the exercise of force to maintain both the statist economies and the accompanying political order (Toye 1992). For example, shortly after independence new political elites sought to consolidate their fragile hold on power and suppress potential contenders. The fragility of the new regimes led political leaders to seek strategic alliances with economic elites of the colonial period, often resulting in suppression of political parties, groups of civil society and unions. Ruling parties and elite groups relied on clientelism, a system of benefits distribution designed to buy the support of political supporters at all levels of society. Where unquestioned support for the ruling party was not forthcoming, party insiders would withdraw economic and social benefits, and often institute political repression. Through this control, the political elite also used its access to wealth as the basis for building its own entrepreneurial roots, creating private corporations capitalized through private appropriation of resource rents.

In summary, basic features of the authoritarian regimes constructed in sub-Saharan Africa in the years following independence, among them Tanzania, Zambia and Zimbabwe, included the following elements:

- domination of political life by a political elite and highly-centralized decision-making bodies;
- suppression of civil society, political parties and workers' organizations;

- marginalization of the peasantry from political processes except for specific political uses;
- distribution of benefits (economic and other) through a system of patronage and clientelism that required fealty to the political elites; and
- use of nationalist or socialist ideology to unify the public against external threats and 'internal enemies'.

(Un)Intended Political Impacts of Structural Adjustment

From the 1980s onwards, the World Bank's approach to dealing with the political dimension of economic reforms has run the full gamut of orientations, beginning with denial of the political impacts of structural change, then acceptance of the political complexities of economic reforms, on to engagement in the stickiness of national political change, and more recently to a more normative approach of promoting 'good governance'.

In its first approach to the political dimension of adjustment, the Bank viewed the economic reform process as implementation of a neutral set of economic instruments crafted to create more efficient economies, increase productivity and enhance competitiveness. These instruments were designed to increase the general welfare and any costs associated with the reforms were clearly viewed as transitional problems to be compensated for as new economic forces set to work (Toye 1992; Gibbon et al 1991). The neutrality perspective crashed in relatively few short years on the political complexities, and often social upheavals, associated with implementing reforms in sub-Saharan Africa, Latin America and Asia in the late 1980s and early 1990s (Nelson 1989; Mosley et al 1991; Van der Hoeven 1994; Widner 1994).

It was also at this juncture in the early 1990s that autocratic regimes in sub-Saharan Africa experienced a democratic turn, giving rise to debate within the Bank and the academic community alike about the relative merits of working with autocratic rulers or democratizing regimes. The Bank's embrace of President Kaunda of Zambia in the late 1980s provides an excellent example of the Bank's conviction that once autocratic rulers had been won over to the need to implement economic reforms, they could achieve quicker, more sweeping results than democratizing political systems (Bratton 1994; Gulhati 1989). However, once Kaunda and his autocratic counterparts in other countries failed to deliver the desired economic outcomes, and resistance from the public intensified in many adjusting countries, the Bank began wrestling with the proposition that newly democratizing regimes might offer better opportunities to implement reforms. This new perspective argued that newly elected leaders had a political mandate, often derived from emerging multi-party political systems, to drive the reform process.

But unstable democratic regimes, as yet uncertain of the scope of their mandates and subject to pressures from many interest groups, were likewise unpredictable partners in implementing economic reforms. Moreover, issues not directly related to adjustment policies, issues for instance having to do with social equity, urban–rural dynamics, and the role of various social, ethnic and cultural groups, also became part of a broader political dynamic that escaped the logic and control of the designers and implementers of adjustment processes in the World Bank. The feeling of being eclipsed by the political realities of the adjustment process was perhaps best captured by then World Bank senior vice-president, Ernie Stern:

> We fail to give full width in our own thinking to the fact that structural adjustment means a major redistribution of economic power and hence of political power in many of the countries undergoing this process. Such a shift is not neutral. It does not happen easily or by itself. The politics of change is one of the reasons adjustment has taken a great deal more time than expected in some countries and one of the reasons some adjustment efforts have not been sustained. I do not believe that the World Bank can do very much about this process except to understand the problem (Stern 1991).

Although a sentiment of resignation settled in among Bank staff when confronted with these complexities at the end of the first decade of adjustment operations, the Bank by no measure ceased to seek ways of pursuing the economic reform programme in coming years. Indeed with some 35 per cent of its lending portfolio invested in policy-based lending, its institutional viability required persistence in finding ways of promoting its reform agenda.

Resistance

Understanding the Bretton Woods institutions' next steps in responding to the political dimension of the economic reform process requires differentiating among the kinds of resistance that took form in developing countries. Resistance in Tanzania, Zambia, Zimbabwe and many other countries in sub-Saharan Africa, and indeed other parts of the world, took two distinct but often overlapping forms. The first form of opposition arose from elite economic and political groups whose positions of power and privilege were clearly threatened by the proposed economic reforms. Losses to elite groups included denial of access to rents, loss of explicit and implicit subsidies, and disruption of oligopolies, non-competitive markets and a host of other economic arrangements that generated private benefit from public resources. Elite groups expressed their opposition through machinations in government and through legislative manoeuvres and decrees. These actors, skilled in the processes of exercising power, succeeded in delaying and often undermining implementation of the economic reforms through internal political manipulation.

The second form of opposition arose from poorer social groups who experienced multiple losses during the adjustment process. The downward pressure on their standards of living came from increases in fees for education and health care, loss of social services, decline in price supports for foodstuffs and, in rural areas, draconian cutbacks in extension, marketing and credit services. Services designed to open the door to social and economic opportunities also suffered under economic retrenchment. In addition, laid-off government employees, often numbering in the tens of thousands, added to the ranks of the new poor in early stages of the adjustment process. Opposition from the urban and, occasionally, rural poor was expressed through direct street action. Urban protests, often organized by labour movements and laid-off government workers, involved strikes, street protests and boycotts and sought to disrupt the functioning of government and the economy. These usually lasted for relatively short periods of time. The rural poor, out of sight and out of the formal political process, usually suffered the downward pressures on their living standards without effective means of protest.

The way elites manipulated and, when necessary, defended themselves against public resistance to the economic reforms differed from country to country. Often, however, elites were able to use public resistance to strengthen their own opposition to structural reforms. Through political manipulation, political elites used mass protests of the poor to derail and postpone implementation of structural change for many years, a history well documented by non-governmental organizations, the World Bank and others (Nelson 1989; Thomas 1991; Mosley et al 1991; Widner 1994). It is important, nonetheless, to remember that despite the political management of public protest, the class interests behind the opposition to economic reforms were fundamentally different.

Enter the Technocrats

Despite their economic might, the Bretton Woods institutions often found they had relatively little influence in resolving conflicts internal to the adjusting countries. In fact, more blatant coercive measures, including muscled conditionalities attached to structural adjustment programmes of the International Monetary Fund and Bank, often proved counterproductive since national elites would stir populist sentiment by condemning the assault by international creditors on national sovereignty. These obstacles to implementing the first generation of adjustment loans gave rise to a second generation of policy-based lending. Learning from previous mistakes, second generation programmes often originated within government agencies before being submitted formally to the Bretton Woods institutions for negotiation, a marked contrast to the earlier process. This new approach to developing reform programmes was predicated on resolving internal struggles among elites and policy makers before seeking support from the international financial community.

A critical ingredient in the success of the second generation adjustment programme was the emergence of 'technopols', that is 'economic technocrats who assume positions of political responsibility' and who are 'motivated to pursue the objectives postulated by traditional normative economic analysis' (Williamson 1994). Slowly but steadily over the two-decade period, the technocrats replaced the previous generation of politicians and policy makers who had been reluctant to embrace the reform programmes. These new decision makers understood the requisites of the international financial institutions and implemented the economic policies required for gaining access to sorely needed financial resources. These new technocrats wrote the economic policies required by the Bretton Woods institutions from within national governments, brokered the agreements with those international agencies, and then assumed responsibility for implementing them, knowing that they did so with the support of the international lenders.

In such manner over the course of the 1990s, the Bank, the European Commission and bilateral donors changed some elements of the process, timing, sequencing and thereby 'ownership' of structural reforms. Through this modified approach, they also increased the probability of successful implementation of economic reform programmes. It is important to point out that this change in the actors in policy formulation on the national level did not change the content of the reform programmes themselves. The fundamental requisites remained intact, requiring that governments remove barriers to the flow of capital, goods and services, and that countries adopt export-oriented growth strategies and decrease significantly the economic role of the state.

Good Governance

With the technocrats and new approach in place and with less political resistance to disrupt the reform programmes, the World Bank and other international development agencies began addressing the political dimensions of economic change through promotion of the principles of 'good governance'. For the IMF and World Bank, the centrepiece of good governance as stated by Mr Camdessus, previous IMF managing director, was to 'maximize the transparency of government financial operations and create systems that minimize the scope for making decisions on an ad hoc basis and for giving preferential treatment to individuals and organizations' (1999). Those principles have served as the basis for engaging governments in the political reform process and, where deemed appropriate, for denying governments access to the international community's financial resources.

In this more neutral approach, the economic policy objectives of the World Bank, summarized in the three points below, converged in such a way as to create market-based economic structures while facilitating the transition to more democratic societies.

- End monopolistic control of key economic sectors. Policies were designed to break up state and private monopolies, liberalize key sectors of the economy and marketing arrangements, and open financial markets to domestic and foreign capital. These non-negotiable reforms were essential to breaking the state's control over the economy.
- Diminish public rent seeking and encourage market-based wealth accumulation. This objective was to be accomplished by privatizing parastatals, dismantling marketing boards, opening markets to private investors and a host of other reforms that would eliminate the capture of rents by government agencies. These economic reforms were intended to unleash market forces, increase efficiency and competitiveness of producers, encourage many new market entrants (both domestic and foreign), and thereby generate an economic dynamism that could not be controlled by state dictates.
- Alter the internal terms of trade to increase the importance of the rural areas relative to the urban sector. This objective was to be accomplished through a series of fiscal reforms to reduce subsidies for urban workers, remove implicit and explicit taxes on agricultural goods, increase investments to strengthen production in the agricultural sector, and improve delivery of services to rural populations, among others.

- With good governance providing the public rationale, the Bretton Woods institutions held that these market-based economic reforms would lead to or, at a minimum, contribute to political democratization in African countries. These economic changes would necessarily increase competition among many economic agents and groups and would thus require that political leaders create more transparent mechanisms for resolving conflicts among competing groups and interests. As a critical mass of competing economic groups emerged, it was further assumed that centralized forms of decision making would no longer be adequate to manage the new economic and political dynamism.

This concept of good governance promoted by the World Bank and IMF establishes a significantly different relationship between markets and the state. In the context of the neoliberal[1] economic reforms, the state is subordinate to the market, serving to put in place the institutions and regulatory regime required for the operation of market economies. Gone from this perspective is recognition that good governance transcends ensuring the transparency and stability of economic interactions. For example, missing is the recognition that good governance involves establishing publicly agreed societal priorities and strategies that oblige markets to serve established goals, goals that include promoting equality of opportunity. Gone from the Bank and Fund perspective is the sense of autonomy of the state and reciprocal complementarity between the state and markets. In short, the Bretton Woods institutions' perspective reduces state functions to providing those services that will facilitate the expansion of the neoliberal economic order and, thereafter, to regulate market activities but not to condition market behaviour to promote broader societal objectives (Comeliau 1998).

NATURAL RESOURCE WEALTH: OLD CHALLENGES IN THE NEW MILLENNIUM

Before examining the impact of the Bretton Woods institutions' approach to dismantling statist economic regimes and political authoritarianism in Tanzania, Zambia and Zimbabwe, we would like to highlight several issues relating to natural resource wealth that were seldom addressed by the reform process. For, despite many changes in the global economy, the fact remains that many countries of sub-Saharan Africa must still address some of the same basic structural and political challenges today that they confronted at the beginning of the decolonization period some 50 years ago.

Continued Dependence on Natural Resource Wealth

Despite the decades of reforms designed to increase efficiency and reduce economic distortions, the countries of sub-Saharan Africa remain as dependent on natural resource wealth as decades ago. For example, agricultural production constitutes 17.8 per cent of aggregate production of the region, rising as high as 99 per cent of GDP in Burkina Faso and above 80 per cent in countries including Malawi (89 per cent), Burundi (88 per cent), Uganda (82 per cent) and Equatorial Guinea (81 per cent). In Tanzania agricultural production comprises 47.6 per cent of GDP, in Zimbabwe 19.5 per cent, and in Zambia 17.3 per cent (World Bank 2000).

Natural resource wealth acquires additional significance when we consider the degree of dependence of those countries on commodity exports. A World Bank study identifies 34 countries from the region that rely on three or fewer commodities to generate more than half their countries' export revenues (Akiyama et al 2001). Ten of those countries rely on only one commodity to generate their hard currency earnings in export markets. Among those countries, Zambia relies on copper to generate virtually the entirety of its export earnings. Zimbabwe relies on export of tobacco, nickel and cotton to generate the bulk of the country's export earnings. Tanzania, though equally reliant on commodity exports, has a somewhat broader range of minerals and agricultural commodities from which hard currency revenues are generated.

Terms of Trade and Market Fluctuations

While data on commodity export dependence provide a snapshot of the importance of natural resources to countries' economic wellbeing, a more complete picture is provided by adding data on trends in actual revenues generated by commodity exports. In this regard, African countries have experienced considerable setbacks over past decades. Terms of trade, an index used 'to measure a commodity-exporting country's ability to pay for capital goods manufactured in developed countries' (Akiyama et al 2001), have worked consistently against the countries of sub-Saharan Africa. While export volumes have increased significantly, oftentimes doubling relative to 1980 when adjustment programmes began, prices have declined steadily. Analysis by the IMF and World Bank provides an succinct summary of this trend:

> Since their short-lived recovery in 1984, real non-oil commodity prices have fallen by about 45 per cent, translating into a sharp deterioration in the terms of trade for most commodity-dependent exporters. In 1992 the price of non-oil commodities relative to that of manufactures reached its lowest level in over 90 years. This pattern in commodity prices has important practical implications for policy makers. For example, the presence of a negative trend in commodity prices implies continuously worsening terms of trade for many commodity-dependent countries, and further, those efforts to stabilize the incomes of producers for an extended period of time may not be financially sustainable (Borensztein et al 1994).

For several reasons, the supply of agricultural goods, particularly from developing countries, increased significantly in the second half of the 1990s. This supply increase was 'widespread and not confined to a few commodities or a few countries' (World Bank 1999). The Bretton Woods institutions attribute the surge in supply and the accompanying decline in prices to three basic factors: efficiency gains associated with policy reforms in developing countries, technological innovation in both agricultural production and mining, and agricultural policies of the

European Union and the United States. The World Bank states the following: 'The largest supply increases have been in the developing countries, where the policies to liberalize markets and privatize production appear to have paid off in higher production' (World Bank 1999).

The impact of that secular trend has been profound, as the IMF's study explains:

It is to be expected that the decline in commodity prices will have its largest impact on countries with the least diversified production structure. Primary commodities still account for the bulk of exports in many developing countries. Moreover, this group of countries, which encompasses many of the lowest-income countries in the world, tends to have less flexible economic systems, making substitution away from commodity production more difficult or costly. In effect, the reliance on primary commodities as the main source of export earnings has only slightly diminished for many countries, particularly in Africa, where manufactures often account for less than 15 percent of merchandise exports (Borensztein et al 1994).

The World Bank's analytical work substantiates the importance of declining terms of trade, stating that, on average, those adverse conditions generated an annual income loss of approximately 1 per cent per year, translating into more than a 20 per cent deterioration over the two-decade period (World Bank 1994). While other more diversified economies were able to absorb these losses, the fairly simple, commodity-dependent economies of the region experienced far more serious setbacks. For example, among the countries included in this study, Zimbabwe actually has experienced aggregate improvements in terms of trade over the past 20 years. That improvement is attributable primarily to the fact that Zimbabwe has a broader manufacturing sector, and consequently the composition of its exports includes significantly more manufactured goods. Zambia and Tanzania, in contrast, experienced significant economic setbacks in export earnings owing in large part to their commodity-export dependence (Akiyama et al 2001).

The impacts of natural resource wealth on the economies of the region, however, are not limited strictly to the declining terms of trade. Numerous studies highlight the difficulties experienced by many countries when commodity prices rise significantly and generate unanticipated government revenues (World Bank 1989; Akiyama et al 2001). As reflected in the experiences of Nigeria, Côte d'Ivoire and Zambia, among other countries, windfalls from commodity price increases (oil, cocoa, coffee, copper) led governments to embark on ambitious investment projects, expand government employment and service provision, and undertake extensive infrastructure programmes. While those ambitious programmes generated considerable domestic political support at the outset, subsequent price collapses brought serious negative economic and political consequences that required years, even decades, to overcome. With declining revenues, governments were unable to shoulder the recurrent costs associated with those ambitious endeavours, which led to rising fiscal deficits, failed investments and cutbacks in public sector employment. The insurmountable debt overhang of more than a few African countries can be tied to the boom-and-bust cycles of commodity prices.

Natural Resource Wealth and Rent Seeking

Efforts to dismantle state rent-seeking activities and to develop market-based economies did not address rent seeking by private agents. Economic rents are above-average benefits accruing to sellers of goods and services. In a sense, rent-seeking and -producing activities are to be found everywhere in market economies, whether through public utility monopolies, patents or intellectual property. In a competitive market, however, one with effective regulatory mechanisms and abundant capital, rents are usually short-lived as new producers or government regulations limit monopolistic practices, and new competition and innovation neutralize the benefits of monopolies.

Monopoly production and state rent seeking became predominant features of the economy in many African countries. However, even if the state is removed from the equation, rent-producing opportunities remain equally abundant unless other changes, both structural and institutional, occur which reduce rent-seeking opportunities for other economic actors. Specifically, rent seeking by private companies can continue unabated unless a very strong regulatory framework and competitive markets are in place.

Structural reforms did not address this issue of private rent seeking in resource-based economies. In fact, the policy prescriptions of the Bretton Woods institutions frequently promoted incentive structures designed to attract foreign capital by providing exceptional opportunities to obtain monopoly rents. They failed to ensure that competitive markets and adequate institutional scaffolding were in place to regulate new investors when they helped design attractive fiscal incentives pro-grammes, exchange rate policies and tariff regimes to entice foreign investors.

The IMF authored a 1999 study, *Does Mother Nature Corrupt? Natural Resources, Corruption, and Economic Growth*, which analyses how 'natural resources might affect a country's economic growth, ie, through an increase in rent-seeking activities' (Leite and Weidmann 1999). The study arrives at several important conclusions, foremost of which is to affirm that 'capital intensive natural resources [ie fuel and ores] are a major determinant of corruption'. Equally significant, the authors assert unambiguously that their findings 'corroborate the negative growth effect of corruption and support our initial hypothesis of the corruption channel being an important explanation for the slow growth of resource-rich economies'.

The concluding paragraphs of the IMF's study merit particular attention, given their relevance to the issues addressed in this publication.

Both our theoretical and empirical results stress the importance of strong (or at least strengthened) institutions in the wake of natural resource discoveries as a way to curb the associated nega-tive growth effects of corruption. This is especially true in less developed countries where natural resource discoveries have a much higher relative impact on both the capital stock and the extent of corruption, and are confronted with generally weaker and less adaptable institutions. Other interesting empirical

results are the findings that, ceteris paribus, neither the corruption
nor the growth process are different in Africa than elsewhere,
and that rapid growth induces an increase in corruption.

While corruption dynamics in African countries are similar to those
registered in other regions, the fact remains that there are far more
African countries dependent on natural resource wealth than in other
regions. Of the 57 countries highly dependent on three leading commodities, 34, or 60 per cent of the total, are in Africa while only nine are
in Asia and 14 in Latin America (Akiyama et al 2001). The point to be
made is that Africa's heavier dependence on natural resource is an important factor in explaining why corruption associated with natural resources
is a problem requiring particular attention in so many African countries.

Looking beyond this discussion of corruption, however, the basic
issue not addressed by the reform process was how resource rents were to
be managed following implementation of economic reforms so as to
raise living standards of the country as a whole and, specifically, to reduce
poverty. Simply replacing an inefficient public monopoly with a more
efficient, even ruthless, private monopoly did not and will not respond
to the needs of resource-based economies trying to increase overall public
welfare through economic reforms.

Challenges for Civil Society

The expansion of the number of groups constituting civil society in
developing countries and their growing influence is linked in many ways
to the failure of the neoliberal economic system to address the social and
environmental dimensions of development. Among the particular challenges facing civil society in countries in sub-Saharan Africa is addressing
the use and distribution of natural resource wealth. As the three country
experiences analysed below demonstrate, the dynamic between economic restructuring and political reforms in resource-based economies is
a volatile and unpredictable process. Perhaps the most central issue in
shaping both economic and political outcomes of the reform process is
the issue of which groups and individuals will gain control over natural
resource wealth.

From our point of view, one of the most important criteria for measuring the success of structural reforms is whether the reforms have increased or eroded the control and access of the poor, particularly the rural poor, to natural resource wealth in its many forms. We focus on that criterion not because the rural poor are necessarily the best custodians of natural resources, although in many societies around the world traditional systems of resource management have proved superior to modern approaches. Rather, it is our view that unless the rural poor have control over adequate resource wealth, they frequently are driven to exert excessive pressure on their resources, contributing to declining productivity and environmental degradation. The consequences of that dynamic, as seen in the three country essays, range far beyond the traditional areas of impoverishment by creating economic, social and environmental problems with serious consequences at the national level (Reed 2001).

On that count, despite many promises, the reform process has created increasingly adverse conditions for the rural poor, engaging them in an economic and institutional reform process over which they have no control. Those adverse conditions today shape the challenges facing civil society in southern African countries in trying to use the region's extensive natural resource wealth to improve living standards and promote sustainable development.

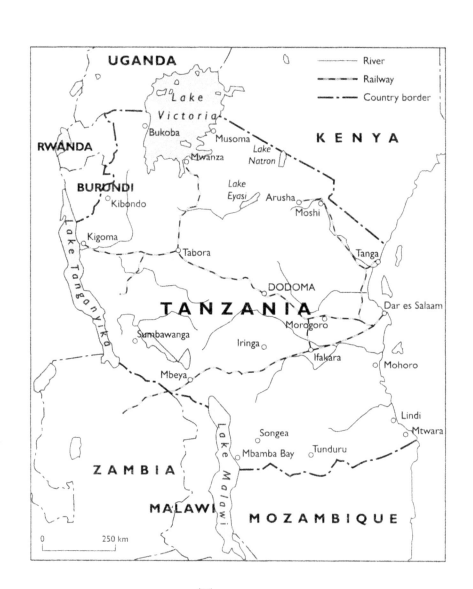

TANZANIA

Chapter 2

Tanzania

*With Dr Kassim Kulindwa**

In no African country did a post-colonial regime attempt to control the economy as completely as did the Tanganyika African National Union (TANU, later renamed Chama Cha Mapinduzi (CCM)), the country's ruling party, from the early 1960s to the mid-1980s. As summarized in one analysis, 'Tanzania's uniqueness lies in the fact that the economic interventionism and government control over the economy were uncommonly direct and comprehensive' (Sarris and Van den Brink 1994). That effort to control and direct the economy extended, by necessity, to the natural resource base of this East African country. TANU/CCM matched its efforts to control economic development with equally comprehensive measures to fragment and dominate the country's civil society, penetrating virtually every civic, labour and religious organization during the period.

* Dr Kassim Kulindwa is senior research fellow and lecturer in economics at the Economic Research Bureau, University of Dar es Salaam. He has co-authored numerous publications including works on structural adjustment, the mining and tourism sectors, and biodiversity in Tanzania. He received his MA from the University of British Columbia and his PhD in economics from the University of Gothenburg.

Although the proclaimed goals of Tanzanian socialism or *Ujamaa* – equity, participation and self-reliance – generated domestic and international support in the years immediately following independence in 1961, the failure to improve the welfare of the country's poor in ensuing decades ultimately led to the collapse of that model of African socialism. While still clinging to the values and ideology articulated by the 1967 Arusha Declaration, and often to its dysfunctional institutional arrangements as well, the country embarked in 1986 on an economic restructuring process that has lasted over a decade and a half but, to date, has failed to alleviate pervasive poverty, particularly in rural areas. While committed in principle to the neoliberal economic policies that underlie global economic integration, the country still seeks to articulate a national development vision. As stated by one observer,

> If the reform process has been guided by a vision, it has been that of the international community. This is not to say that there has not been national support for reforms, but that acceptance has so far fallen short of the definition of a new set of clear national goals to replace those articulated in the Arusha Declaration (Van Arkadie 1995).

Natural resource wealth lies at the centre of the economic reform programme being implemented in Tanzania. First and foremost, the reform programme has sought to remove the state from its commanding position in organizing agricultural production in order to provide new incentives and opportunities to small farmers and agribusiness alike. Complementing agricultural sector and land reforms, mining and tourism sectors also have been central to the restructuring of the economy and have become the fastest growing sectors of the economy during the past decade. Reforms in mining and tourist industries have placed emphasis on attracting foreign capital to drive expansion of these natural resource sectors. As summarized below, that approach has unleashed many new economic agents and created new dynamics, resulting in economic gains but also environmental, social and political difficulties for the country.

The key issues that Tanzania's experience raises regard the regulatory framework and institutional mechanisms that have accompanied the economic reforms. First, the experience highlights the outcomes resulting from a deficient regulatory system, a system that has little authority or inclination to staunch rampant rent-seeking behaviour. Second, the experience underscores the social and environmental costs of conflicts between local communities and the new economic agents unleashed by the reform process. Third, the essay highlights how these outcomes are tied to institutional arrangements by which the actions of an economic and political elite lie well beyond public scrutiny, weakening confidence in both the economic reforms and political order.

We begin this essay by reviewing why the failed agrarian socialist model obliged the Tanzanian government to embark on sweeping economic reforms in the 1980s, and then summarize the economic programme designed to reverse the country's downward spiral. Second, we examine how the reform measures affected three basic facets of the natural resource-based economy: land, minerals and tourism assets. Our essay reviews the important contributions of the economic gains associated with these sectors and thereafter highlights a number of key issues that jeopardize the sustainability of the country's development path and pose serious problems to ensuring public accountability of economic actors in coming years.

THE IMPERATIVES OF CHANGE

Agrarian Socialism and Authoritarianism

Within two years of independence in 1961, President Julius Nyerere declared that Tanganyika 'should become a constitutional one-party state' in the interest of national unity and economic development. In its first efforts to establish a political monopoly, the ruling party, TANU, abolished traditional chieftaincies that governed rural areas and similarly banned ethnic organizations from participating in national political affairs. Thereafter, the new party elite outlawed strikes and compelled independent trade unions, the organizational foundation of the liberation struggle, to affiliate with union structures created and controlled by the party (Baregu 1994). Similarly, following a failed mutiny in 1964, a new army was formed under TANU control (Bienen 1978). Through these and parallel repressive measures, the ruling party transformed Tanganyika into a one-party state that allowed little political dissent and little room for economic initiative and entrepreneurial experimentation. That same year witnessed the unification of Tanganyika and Zanzibar into the United Republic of Tanzania (URT).

In the context of this increasingly autocratic regime, President Nyerere introduced the Arusha Declaration in 1967 to establish *Ujamaa* and villagization as the foundations of the country's development strategy. That historic proclamation articulated the strictures of African socialism through concepts of equity, participation and self-reliance. Rather than embracing an industrialization model, as had other socialist states, Tanzanian socialism articulated a vision of an agrarian society that would guarantee a modest but secure standard of living for all members of society. This model seemed particularly well adapted to Tanzania, where 90 per cent of the population lived in rural areas, earning approximately US$180 per year (Weaver and Anderson 1981).

TANU established agriculture as the leading sector to drive its national development strategy, as articulated in the new government's First Five Year Plan, 1964–69. That plan was built on two operational pillars: improvement and transformation. Under improvement, the government would play an activist role in providing extension services, marketing and credit to small farmers. With transformation, the government would attempt to promote capital- and input-intensive agriculture, initially on a pilot basis, by creating large-scale village settlement programmes. In the years immediately following independence, this economic approach adopted by the ruling party actually increased agricultural productivity by 4 per cent and GDP growth by more than 6 per cent per annum. While overall sectoral policies proved favourable, initial villagization efforts did not generate positive economic results (Sarris and Van den Brink 1994).

Disregarding the economic failure of prototype *Ujamaa* villages, the ruling party moved forward with villagization as the strategic linchpin of Tanzania's agrarian socialism. Between 1974 and 1976 forced villagization obliged more than half of the country's population to move into *Ujamaa* villages. The public rationale held that by concentrating the rural population into central villages, economies of scale could be achieved, technical improvements could be shared widely, credit could be offered more broadly and centralized marketing could ensure access of rural producers to markets. Moreover, geographic concentration of the population would ensure delivery of social services to greater numbers of peasants while also cutting delivery costs. To this rationale was added the ideological imperative of combating the evils of exploitive economic practices, including simple rural wage labour. Rural capitalists and Asian and Arab commercial groups that had benefited under colonial rule were among the main targets of statist economic control (Msambichaka et al 1994).

With this social and economic rationale, TANU, which became CCM in 1977, constructed an economy that virtually excluded private initiative in agriculture and other sectors. Smallholders were grouped into *Ujamaa* villages through which state institutions managed all aspects of their economic and political lives. Large and medium agriculture enterprises were nationalized and reorganized as parastatals, allowing private estate production only in areas such as Arusha and Kilimanjaro where producers managed to fend off state efforts to control their production (Sarris and Van den Brink 1994). Economic institutions dominating the agricultural sector included a three-tiered marketing system controlled by the government, credit-making institutions managed by the central bank, fertilizer and input distribution systems, fixed input and product prices and a tightly regulated foreign exchange system. Through these mechanisms the state was able to capture the profits and rents of the agricultural sector.

The ruling party also established the legal and institutional mechanisms by which the political elite controlled the lands on which national economic fortunes depended. The terms of land ownership under the party were actually established under colonial rule by the *Land Ordinance* of 1923 that vested ownership and control of all lands in the state. The Arusha Declaration and accompanying *Rural Lands Act* of 1973 granted the state the authority to declare any part of the national territory a 'specified area', meaning the government could dispose of land as it deemed appropriate. While these measures recognized customary titles and allowed for village jurisdiction, villages were never granted ownership of the land, a right also denied to individuals living in those rural areas.

During those two decades of experimentation with agrarian socialism, neither mining nor tourism was accorded importance in the country's development strategy. The mining sector was nationalized in the early days following independence and all mining activities were centralized under the State Mining Corporation (STAMICO). The few large-scale mining activities, including the Buck Reef Gold Mine in Geita, soon stagnated from poor management and lack of government investment. The ledger sheet for the period shows a dismal economic return on state investment and a total withdrawal of private capital from the sector (Chachage 1995). Despite the formation of the Tanzania Tourist Corporation (TTC), created by the new government to promote tourism in the post-independence period, this economic sector was largely disregarded since tourism was viewed as antithetical to socialist ideals.

In summary, the political elite organized wealth accumulation in Tanzania during the country's first 20 years through the following mechanisms.

- The state organized and dominated smallholder production as the principal mechanism for wealth accumulation. All inputs, credit, technological innovations, transportation and marketing arrangements were controlled by state agencies.
- The state appropriated and managed the majority of large and medium agricultural enterprises and eliminated most opportunities for private capital accumulation and export agriculture.
- Monopoly by the state of all other economic sectors complemented domination of agriculture, the economy's leading sector. Transfers from the agricultural sector supported import-substitution industrialization while economic opportunities, such as expanding tourism and mining, were disregarded. Industrialization strategy sought to achieve a wildly optimistic goal of industrial self-sufficiency in all basic sectors within a 20-year period.

Structural Change and the Natural Resource Sectors

Overcoming Resistance

By 1980, two decades after independence, Tanzanian policy makers could not escape the imperative to embark on sweeping economic change. The country's GDP had declined steadily since 1975, and between 1981 and 1982 the annual growth rate dropped from 2.1 per cent to 0.6 per cent. Industrial output contracted by 20 per cent annually and agricultural production continued its steady decline during the early 1980s (Sarris and Van den Brink 1994). Sixty per cent of the population was living below the poverty line, with a high proportion of the poor living in rural areas. While investment in social infrastructure helped raise Tanzania to 34th position in the United Nations Development Programme's Human Development Index, the country had the world's second lowest GDP per capita (World Bank 1996).

There is little doubt that adverse external conditions played a significant part in the country's economic collapse in 1980. Global recession in the mid-1970s; the break-up of the East Africa Community, in which Tanzania was a central player, in 1977; the doubling of oil prices between 1979 and 1980; and the war with Uganda between 1978 and 1979, coupled with two crippling droughts, generated steady external shocks for the fragile economy. However, the failed policies of *Ujamaa* had sapped the economy of its post-independence vitality and further deepened policy makers' inability to respond to adverse external conditions. The state-controlled agricultural sector, a highly inefficient, state-dominated industrial sector, and marketing arrangements dominated by the state marketing boards all drained scarce financial resources and created economic disincentives throughout the economy.

The country's natural resource base also experienced serious degradation between independence and the implementation of economic reforms some 25 years later. Forced villagization has been identified as one of the major disruptive factors in Tanzania's rural ecology. Concentrating agricultural production in densely populated areas instead of maintaining the dispersed productive arrangements prior to *Ujamaa* led to deforestation, decline in soil fertility and extensive erosion (Shechambo and Kulindwa 1995). Clearing forested lands for agriculture and satisfying the country's need for fuel, 90 per cent of which came from wood sources, led to the loss of 25 per cent of Tanzania's forests. The resulting exposure of fragile soils to wind and water erosion resulted in annual rates of soil loss as high as 55 tons per hectare. Poaching and habitat destruction during the 1980s resulted in the loss of 290,000 elephants. Tanzania also suffered urban air pollution, coastal erosion, water pollution, mangrove clearing, reef damage from dynamite fishing and uncontrolled development of tourist hotels (Kulindwa et al 2000b).

Many policy makers strongly resisted implementing structural change throughout the 1980s and remained particularly hostile to embarking on policy reforms relying on financial support, and accompanying conditionalities, from the Bretton Woods institutions. This resistance led the government to attempt an initial economic reform process through a domestically designed and financed adjustment programme, the National Economic Survival Programme of 1981. The programme failed to resolve basic price and policy distortions in the agricultural sector and soon obliged the government to adopt a more severe economic programme in 1982. Included in that programme were components that sought to bring burgeoning government deficits under control and to improve the performance of parastatals (Gibbon 1995; World Bank 1996).

Those timid measures did little to staunch the country's economic problems and, in fact, the government's refusal to adopt more stringent IMF reforms led many foreign donors, on which the economy was becoming increasingly dependent, to withhold financial support. Rising inflation, declining productivity, falling hard currency revenues, all fuelling a new inflationary cycle, intensified economic problems to the point that the government had little option but to seek agreement with the IMF in 1986. The resulting Economic Recovery Plan gave strong emphasis to currency devaluation and trade liberalization as the first steps toward opening the economy to foreign investment. The IMF-supported stabilization plan was followed several years later by the second phase of the adjustment process, a World Bank programme,

Economic and Social Adjustment Programme (ESAP), that gave particular attention to liberalizing foreign investment regulations and deepening reforms in the agricultural sector while also addressing the social costs associated with adjustment.

The third phase of Tanzania's adjustment programme, the Rolling Plan and Forward Budget of 1993, gave priority to reforming the civil service and privatizing the public sector. Government downsizing, including reductions of over 50,000 in the numbers of civil servants between 1993 and 1995, was central to reducing the government's mounting debt burden. Similarly, privatization of the more than 400 parastatals began in earnest during this period, although another five years would be required to fulfill many of the divestiture objectives (Gibbon 1995; Bol et al 1997).

Restructuring the Agricultural Sector

The overarching objective of reforms in the agricultural sector was to dismantle state control of production and marketing in order to, first, encourage private initiative and create opportunities for small farmers and, second, to attract national and foreign investment in medium and large commercial farming. Given that agriculture still accounted for approximately 50 per cent of Tanzania's GDP and provided livelihoods for 80 per cent of the population, structural changes in this sector held the key to success of reforms in other sectors, particularly natural resource sectors.

The starting point of the reform programme was replacing the government's administered price regime with a market-based pricing system. Success in accomplishing that goal was steady. By 1991, the reform programme lifted price controls on all but nine items out of a total of over 3000 in 1978 (Sarris and Van den Brink 1994; Bol et al 1997). As the government's three-tiered, one-channel marketing arrangement was slowly liberalized and as competition from private competitors slowly increased, a substantial supply response for food crops also followed. However, as the government wanted to control foreign currency revenues, liberalization of export crops proceeded at a pace much slower than that promoted by the Bretton Woods institutions and resulted in depressed output for a protracted period.

By 1995 the continuing efforts to liberalize the agricultural sector allowed for a growth rate of over 5 per cent per annum. Still, agricultural exports were lower in mid-1996 than they were in the late 1960s and overall sectoral productivity remained lower than in many less developed countries (World Bank 1996). Moreover, expanded sectoral output resulted largely from the expansion of cultivated areas, not from technification or intensification. These problems led the government and World Bank to shift priorities from implementing additional structural changes, that is, from deepening liberalization, to addressing structural constraints that inhibited productivity gains particularly among small farmers. Included in those constraints are limited rural infrastructure, limited educational opportunities and a limited capacity to provide technical inputs that could encourage crop diversification and increase access to export markets (Shechambo and Kulindwa 1995; World Bank 1997a, 1997b).

The government and international agencies have recognized that redefining the tenurial foundations of agricultural production is central to Tanzania's growth path. To that end, priority is being given to ensuring that the 3.5 million smallholders, who now cultivate 4.1 million hectares of land, secure access to their main productive asset. Moreover, redistribution of state-owned agricultural lands, totalling 2 million hectares under the control of 730 parastatal farms, to small and medium landholders will also be vital in increasing economic prospects for the millions of rural poor.

Thus far, efforts to increase local ownership have been central to the development of a new National Land Policy (NLP), which is viewed as a dynamic and indispensable part of the new economic regime. The NLP and enabling legislation continue to vest all land in the President as trustee of the people, an extension of the colonial era Land Ordinance of 1923. However, in the context of increased support for individual land ownership and titling, the policy allows individuals to hold titles to land not dedicated to communal use, land conservation or other village activities. Still, administration and decision making at the communal level remain unclear in many aspects and several issues relating to use of pastoral and common resource areas likewise remain to be clarified. Moreover, the biggest challenge to implementing the land reform remains developing the government's administrative capacity to ensure accuracy, fairness and expediency in implementing the reform process that is already beset by complex and conflicting interests among many parties (World Bank 1996).

Despite these limitations and conflicts, structural and institutional changes have fundamentally altered the economic regime under which the government controlled agricultural production, captured rents from the rural sector and maintained its autocratic control over Tanzanian society. The principal challenge now resides in allocating financial resources through which the infrastructure, inputs, credit and education required to increase productivity can be provided. Allocation of these resources will play a deciding role in determining who will be the long-term beneficiaries of the reforms in the agricultural sector: smallholders seeking to rise out of poverty or the medium and large commercial farms which, in addition to having capital, technology and market access, now have a legal and tenurial structure within which they can freely operate.

Opening the Mining Sector

The third phase of Tanzania's reform programme has had particular importance for the mining and tourism sectors. While the agricultural sector languished under the institutional experimentation of Tanzanian socialism for the better part of 30 years, the CCM recognized by the early 1980s that reforming the mining sector offered prospects for attracting desperately needed foreign investment. After early attempts to stimulate expansion of the sector floundered under parastatal management, the ruling party placed its hope in attracting foreign capital in order to rekindle growth in this potentially dynamic sector. Liberalizing the mining sector would not necessarily conflict with the underlying principles of *Ujamaa* so long as the agricultural sector remained protected from foreign and capitalist influences.

In that context, the CCM promulgated the *Mining Act* of 1979 which, while continuing to vest all ownership in the state, established a framework for granting licences to private ventures for prospecting and mining activities, giving priority to attracting large-scale foreign investment. Thereafter, the Mining Policy Paper of 1983 provided additional opportunities and encouragement to small-scale miners so that they, too, would increase activity in the sector. This act was followed by subsequent legislation, notably the *National Investment and Promotion Act* of 1990, which provided additional incentives to foreign investment by ensuring repatriation of revenues and deregulating marketing arrangements. With the passage of the subsequent Mining Policy of 1998 and *Mining Act* of 1999, liberalization of the sector was complete. The laws established an attractive regulatory framework, provided significant incentives including five-year tax holidays, and guaranteed repatriation of profits for large-scale investors. From these capital-intensive mining operations, the government anticipated generating a steady revenue flow.

It took little over a decade for these new incentives and liberalized economic relations to make mining one of the most dynamic, rapidly growing sectors of the Tanzanian economy. Initially, however, rather than attracting the large-scale investors from which government revenues would flow, three largely unanticipated sectoral changes occurred. Those changes have brought only modest capital for direct investment, have done little to raise the technological level and have contributed minimally to improving government revenue capture from the sector.

First, initial investors were 'mainly interested in the exploitation of trade in minerals, rather than introducing new or more advanced technology' on which genuine large-scale operations could develop (Chachage et al 1993; Chachage 1995). The first major outcome in the sector was the broadening of the highly porous marketing arrangements inherited from years past under which 76 per cent of gold and 80 per cent of gem stones were smuggled out of the country to be marketed in neighbouring countries or centres in Thailand (Kulindwa et al 2000a). This institutional situation allowed existing brokers and merchants, largely of Asian origin, to capture rents from the sector, to shield profits from government fiscal control and, in so doing, to accumulate significant personal wealth, much of it invested offshore.

Second, with the broadening of economic relations, medium-sized claim-holders, brokers and dealers organized the activities of as many as one million small-scale miners who had moved into the sector during the past decade. This complex system of claim-holders and claim-managers organized the new small-scale miners into an integrated, albeit chaotic, system of surveying, prospecting and extracting specific minerals or gem stones. These mid-sized mining companies took advantage of the competing and confusing land tenure systems, imprecise and conflicting regulations, uncertainties of community rights and responsibilities and the poverty of independent miners. They offered working conditions to small miners that provided no contractual stability, offered no fixed prices for gold or gem stones, burdened the miners with most of the risks and made loans for tools and other supplies at usurious rates. These companies complied with no environmental regulations, paid no reparations to local villages for contaminated water, clearing of forests or digging up of agricultural lands and, to a large degree, avoided paying taxes.

Third, an estimated one million small-scale miners moved into this largely unregulated yet very dynamic context during the last decades of the century. Those miners came from all walks of life and all geographic regions of the country (Kulindwa et al 2000a). For example, in the late 1970s and early 1980s a number of gold rushes occurred in various localities, causing small villages to swell by 5000 or even 15,000 migrants in few years. Similar demographic shifts continued in the 1990s. This explosion of mining operations unquestionably generated employment and income for these hundreds of thousands of poor workers. It drew peasants into the money economy, created small-scale industries and services around the mining towns, and allowed many miners to reinvest earnings in their local landholdings.

In the last years of the 1990s this scenario began to change. In addition to the dynamics described above, international mining corporations began investing in the country. Ashanti Goldfields launched a joint gold mining venture with Resolute Limited, an Australian company, and began operations in Nzega in 1998. Kahama Mining Corporation and Barrick of Canada acquired rights to one of the largest gold deposits in East Africa. Randgold Resources of South Africa joined with Pangea Minerals of Canada prospecting for gold. Pangea Minerals also formed a partnership with Anglo-American of South Africa to mine diamonds, and East African Gold Mines Company has expanded its prospecting activities (Kulindwa et al 2000a). These recent ventures have the potential to significantly increase the level of investment, to raise the technology level and to generate a steady revenue stream for the government. Whether these corporations will raise the level of environmental performance, complying with established environmental impact assessment requirements, is a matter of conjecture.

Prior to the entry of the foreign corporations, the economic momentum and demographic movement associated with these widely dispersed mining activities obliged the government at local and regional levels to open lands and grant claims to these individual and loosely organized miners. Since mining claims were often granted by regional authorities far from the affected communities, innumerable conflicts with local authorities arose, and tensions between miners and local villagers erupted. Frequently, no one was certain how to resolve competing claims or reestablish the authority of appropriate government agencies (Chachage 1995; Kulindwa et al 2000a). While the *Land Act* of 1999 and *Village Land Act* of 1999 have superseded many parts of the prior land tenure regime, uncertainties regarding the authority for determining land use and establishing usufruct rights prevent resolution of innumerable land claims between mining companies, small-scale miners and communities.

The environmental costs associated with the expansion of the mining sector have been staggering. Studies in Mererani in Arusha, Geita in Mwanza, and Umba in Tanga indicated widespread water contamination, deforestation, loss of biodiversity and degradation of agricultural fields. Silt, salt, oil, chemicals and tailings are regularly dumped around mining sites large and small. The health consequences for miners and neighbouring villagers are significant, as mercury, graphite, kerosene and faecal matter have quickly found their way into water supplies from surface and groundwater sources. Moreover, the clearing of land for hundreds, often thousands, of migrants' living quarters disrupted communal lands, decimated forests, and polluted watersheds (Kulindwa et al 2000a).

In summary, initial development of the mining sector followed a path not anticipated by the government of Tanzania or the World Bank. Initially, few large-scale mining companies moved into the sector despite the attractive regulatory framework and financial incentives held out to them. In contrast, hundreds of thousands of rural and urban poor found work in mining camps and ancillary small-scale service providers have developed to support their mining activities. Medium-sized mining companies and gemstone merchants occupied dominant positions in the industry, taking full advantage of the new incentives. With the recent entry of some of the world's largest gold and diamond mining companies into Tanzania, dynamics in the sector are set for change. The direction and magnitude of that change is uncertain.

What is clear is that, to date, expansion in the sector has been seriously marred by the lack of an enforceable regulatory framework despite considerable efforts by miners' organizations, and even some government offices, to implement new regulations. As a consequence of the weak regulatory framework, rent seeking by private mining and marketing companies, smuggling of gold and semi-precious stones, and evasion of taxes have become the norm, clearly to the detriment of the government's tax recovery efforts. Moreover, entrenched rent-seeking behaviour has deepened opportunities for collusion between the mining and marketing companies and employees of government agencies who are responsible for granting mining concessions, overseeing collection of tax revenues from marketing companies, and monitoring market entrants and their activities. This deepening collaboration between private interests and public agencies has given risen to public belief that a 'political mafia' is operating in this sector, a group that is controlled by no one and can act with relative impunity in pursuing personal gain.

Expanding Tourism

As with the mining sector, liberalization of the macro economy has created economic conditions under which tourist entrepreneurs have benefited significantly during the past decade. Prior to developing a comprehensive tourism policy in 1991, tourism was promoted on an ad hoc basis by the TTC, a public enterprise which failed to generate either a sectoral development plan or steady revenues. Liberalization of the economy by the 1990s created both economic and ideological conditions under which tourism development could take place. While donor agencies have provided technical and financial support to help develop the sector, an integrated Tourism Development Master Plan was written by government agencies, private consultants and representatives of tour operators. Notably absent in preparing the plan were the local stakeholders who remain responsible for managing local tourist areas.

The formally adopted National Tourism Plan, released in 1991 and revised in 2000, established the mechanisms by which the state's direct economic involvement, primarily involvement during the mid-1980s to upgrade facilities and infrastructure, was to be supplanted by the private sector. In the move to privatize the sector, the government has sought to:

- increase the tourism sector's contribution to national output by increasing foreign exchange earnings, creating new employment opportunities and stimulating development of rural areas and human capital; and
- ensure conservation of tourism attractions, preservation of the environment and long-term development of the tourism sector (Kulindwa et al 2000b).

Attracting foreign investors has been central to the success of the plan over the past decade. For example, the incentives established by the National Tourism Plan provide special benefits to companies based in neighbouring countries, notably Kenya, and to overseas operators, for example by providing tax holidays and exemptions. The government's weak, often non-existent monitoring capacity has also favoured vertical integration of tourist activities under foreign control, an assessment confirmed by the Ministry of Natural Resources and Tourism (URT 2000). The plan also provides additional rewards to large foreign investors who can mobilize large investment packages and establish dominant positions in the emerging industry.

One of the most important, and yet unsettled, issues in developing the tourism sector regards relations between entrepreneurs and local communities, a relation shaped by insecure land tenure and usufruct rights. As with other land-related issues in Tanzania, the *Land Ordinance Act* of 1923 established the basic tenurial rules governing the sector, including the right of the President to appropriate land for tourist hotel construction. Although the National Land Policy (NLP) of 1995, the *Land Act* of 1999 and the *Village Land Act* of 1999 have overridden many aspects of the *Land Ordinance Act* of 1923, all land remains vested in the President. Under the new laws, a dual system of tenure will take effect in which a 'granted right of occupancy' will apply in urban and peri-urban areas while, in rural areas, village councils will continue to administer communal lands.

In principle, the policy supports the concept of 'benefit sharing' among users of wildlife reserves and gives priority to local communities in filling new job opportunities. In addition, wildlife policy encourages all activities to 'involve all stakeholders in wildlife conservation and sustainable utilization, as well as in fair and equitable sharing of benefits'. Regardless of official policy, the current land tenure regime is responsible for creating land disputes in many parts of the country. The essence of those conflicts regards the ability of communities and individuals to control use of lands when tourist enterprises want to expand their operations. Such conflicts persist in areas of high farming density, areas bordering national parks and reserves, and fishing waters, beaches and seaweed farming areas. For example, in Bagamoyo, agricultural and tourist development have increased the scarcity of land available to small farmers. In Bagamoyo and Zanzibar, fishermen have lost access to fishing areas and beaches as a result of the refusal or inability of government agencies to protect the rights of local communities. These conflicts have increased dramatically since the tourism sector was opened to foreign investors.

The situation on the ground is exacerbated by conflicting decision-making mechanisms on national and local levels, and the uncertainty associated with various kinds of ownership claims. Wildlife policy generates its own confusing if not conflicting dynamics because of the uncertainty about rights and responsibilities for managing wildlife, relations between parks and adjoining communities, and the distribution of benefits derived from safari and non-consuming tourist enterprises. These complex dynamics are often intensified by the failure of tour operators to provide employment opportunities to local inhabitants and to distribute revenues through community governance mechanisms (Kulindwa et al 2000b).

As regards environmental problems, coastal tourist developments provide clear examples of ripple effects that often start with the destruction of mangrove forests, estuaries, beaches and coral reefs. Disruption of these areas has created serious negative impacts on surrounding fisheries and has resulted in coastal erosion. Most hotels in Zanzibar and Bagamoyo are built with mangrove poles, and demand for wood for construction in Ngorongoro and Serengeti is rapidly growing as tourist thatched structures proliferate. Tourism increases the demand for handicrafts and other wood products, leading to deforestation in areas around the new tourist sites.

The government's ability to foster sustainable tourism and mining is hampered by several problems. The government's capacity to enforce regulations and policies is severely limited by low levels of staffing, inadequate training, poor communication and substandard tools and facilities. Although coastal hotels, for example, are governed by wastewater treatment requirements, government unwillingness or inability to enforce standards has resulted in extensive water pollution. Employee shortages and funding shortfalls have kept the Wildlife Department from enforcing poaching laws.

Another shortcoming is that Tanzanian policy makers have taken a very centralized approach and have not adequately involved local communities in decisions that affect them. This has led to the creation of laws and institutions that are not responsive to local needs and are often unpopular, and so are not supported. Government institutions often have little representation at the local level, limiting the potential participation of local governments and communities and creating serious communication challenges.

THE ECONOMIC IMPACT OF THE STRUCTURAL REFORMS ON MINING AND TOURISM

Taken on the aggregate level, economic reforms have generated generally positive economic outcomes. For example, real growth averaged 3.3 per cent annually in the reform period of 1987–98. That is a significant improvement when compared to the 1.6 per cent growth rate in years prior to adjustment. Improvement in aggregate figures was reflected in both the mining and tourism sectors. The mining sector's share of GDP increased from 0.8 per cent in 1980 to 1.3 per cent in 1993 and then climbed to 2 per cent in 1998. After years of decline, tourism's share of GDP increased from 1.5 per cent in 1990 to 7.4 per cent in 1998, underscoring its rising importance to the national economy. On the island of Zanzibar alone, tourism's share of total output increased from an average of 10.9 per cent between 1993 and 1995 to an average of 14.1 per cent between 1996 and 1998 (Kulindwa et al 2000a, 2000b).

Taking a second aggregate indicator, the fiscal balance, reforms also improved performance rapidly after 1985, with budget deficits falling from 11 per cent of GDP in 1986 to 4.6 per cent in 1998. Efforts to reduce budget deficits affected development in these two sectors in a number of ways, both positively and negatively. In tourism, for example, the state's withdrawal from the sector, combined with its efforts to provide policy guidance, proved an important stimulus to sectoral growth. However, across the board budget cuts restrained provision of infrastructure development and services in a way that clearly hindered opportunities for expansion of tourism. In 1994 and 1995, government allocations for tourism, natural resources and the environment accounted for only 0.5 per cent of total recurrent expenditures and 3 per cent of the total development budget. The pattern was similar for the late 1990s (Kulindwa et al 2000a, 2000b).

A third aggregate indicator, the country's trade balance, witnessed a steady growth of the trade deficit despite the increase of foreign exchange earnings generated by the mining and tourism sectors. The overall ratio of exports to imports improved from -0.49 in 1980 to -0.29 in 1985, but fell again to -0.53 in 1998. Analysis shows that factors such as declining terms of trade for other exports, notably agricultural commodities, helped boost the overall share of earnings contributed by mining and tourism. Tourism, for example, showed consistent growth in its contribution to total exports. Its share increased from 12 per cent in 1990 to 36 per cent in 1998. Mineral exports also increased, as exemplified by the doubling of gold exports between 1997 and 1998. Diamond and gold continued to be the leading minerals in 1998, contributing 64 per cent of total mineral exports. Analysis demonstrates that contributions of mineral exports to formal aggregate output would have been significantly greater if it were not for illegal cross-border trade. For example, despite substantial tariff reductions and an attractive business environment, an estimated 76 per cent of total gold production and 80 per cent of total gem stone production is traded illegally (Kulindwa et al 2000a, 2000b).

A final aggregate indicator, tax revenues, experienced a downward trend despite the increased tax contributions from both mining and tourism. Prior to reforms of the mid-1990s, the country's tax system was highly porous and encouraged tax evasion and black-market activities through high tax rates, widespread corruption, and poor enforcement. While the tax system has since been improved, the mining industry remains weakly compliant and the government makes little effort to collect revenues from small-scale operations. Revenues from tourism remain significantly below potential. In addition to tax evasion by small operators, the *Tanzania Investment Act* of 1997 included tax incentives for mining and tourism, such as tax holidays, that generated tax revenue losses estimated to equal about US$30 million a year.

The reforms have generated other important economic changes in these two sectors, foremost of which has been the creation of employment opportunities. Estimates of employment created in the 1990s in the mining sector vary widely. A 1996 study conducted by Tan-Discovery, a private company, estimated that more than 555,000 people were directly involved in mining. The Federation of Miners Associations of Tanzania (FEMATA) estimated that 550,000 people were directly engaged in mining activities in 1997 and that by 1999 the number had surged to more than a million. Data on employment creation in tourism are unreliable, but it is safe to assume that employment growth must have accompanied the rapid economic growth of the sector. Tourist visits in Zanzibar rose 136 per cent in the 1980s and 105 per cent between 1990 and 1997. On the mainland, tourism rose 82 per cent in the 1980s and 215 per cent between 1990 and 1998 (Kulindwa et al 2000b). In addition to the many people employed directly in mining and tourism, many others (shopkeepers, farmers, auto mechanics, artisans) are employed in closely related secondary activities.

Earnings from mining and tourism have shown consistent growth. Tourism earnings increased from US$27 million in 1986 to US$570 million in 1998. Revenue gains resulted from increased numbers of tourists as well as increased fees for services. The majority of tourists to Tanzania were attracted to high-value activities, such as game hunting and photo safaris. Earnings from game hunting increased from about US$5.2 million in 1993 to US$8.6 million in 1998.

In summary, economic reforms have had major impacts on these two sectors and have altered their relative contributions to the country's economic balances. Positive outcomes included higher economic growth, an improved fiscal balance, more employment opportunities and increased government revenues.

THE PROMISE OF CONTINUING CHANGE

Benefits and Beneficiaries

Structural reforms have had a significant impact in liberalizing Tanzania's economy and dismantling the state-controlled agrarian socialist system. Foremost among the changes implemented has been the dismantling of centralized control over the agricultural sector. Previous state control sought to channel profits from agriculture to fuel a wildly ambitious 20-year industrialization programme, severely constraining economic opportunities for farmers large and small. With the sector freed from administered prices, the reforms have opened market opportunities to agribusiness as well as millions of smallholders. The *New Land Act* and the *Village Land Act* provide opportunities for increasing access and use of land by the rural poor. Villages can now use village land as collateral to obtain credit for communal endeavours, and women – previously unable to secure land as individuals – can now hold productive land. Potentially, and we must underscore the word 'potentially', impoverished peasants across the Tanzanian countryside stand to benefit from these aspects of the economic reform programme.

Opening natural resources sectors, in particular mining and tourism, to market forces has generated quite mixed, if not conflicting, outcomes.

Since the government had not invested heavily in either mining or tourism, the economic reform programme did not bring about a redistribution of economic control from the state to the private sector. Instead, liberalization has sought to expand private sector activity, particularly by providing targeted incentives to foreign investors.

The government plan to attract large-scale mining by providing ample rent-seeking opportunities did not succeed initially. The entrance of major international mining companies, including Ashanti Goldfields and Anglo-America, changed that scenario at the close of the century. Prior to their entry, other economic actors, particularly medium-sized companies and marketing firms, moved quickly to take advantage of the rent-seeking opportunities and to establish their influence over the sector. They were able to use small miners to prospect potential mining sites, extract gold and gem stones using rudimentary technology, realize significant profits with minimal investment and escape regulatory constraints. Marketing firms expanded their illegal trade in gem stones and gold, avoiding government fiscal control, and generating considerable profits often kept offshore. With the entrance of large corporations to the sector, rent seeking may reach a new level.

Opening of the tourism sector likewise sought to attract foreign companies, who responded with a modest but fairly steady flow of investment capital. The incentives offered to foreign operators provided considerable advantage relative to national companies that did not enjoy similar subsidies and fiscal incentives. That said, new tourism opportunities did arise for local tour operators, who provided services to complement the high quality services offered to a largely foreign tourist clientele.

Despite pervasive institutional and regulatory shortcomings, the macroeconomy benefited from the reforms carried out in these two natural resource sectors. Their contribution to GDP increased, exports increased and employment rose. These are not insignificant macroeconomic outcomes.

Moreover, the half to one million small-scale miners who became active in mining activities derived immediate economic benefits from their move into the sector, despite the vulnerabilities and difficult working conditions. Likewise, a limited number of new employees associated with tourist centres have derived similar economic benefit.

Costs and their Distribution

The social and environmental costs associated with the reforms are quite extensive. We have indicated a number of the immediate costs including extensive degradation of forests, contamination of waters, degradation of agricultural lands and disruption of marine ecosystems, among many others. Consistent failure to invest, and to oblige users to reinvest, in maintaining the integrity of national parks is leading to serious degradation in the quality of tourist destinations.

Social costs include increased conflict between miners and communities, between tour operators and communities, and between government representatives and local communities. Social costs to be paid both individually and socially are the health impacts arising from working in very difficult, toxic conditions and from water and air pollution. Social costs we have not detailed include the rise in HIV/AIDS in mining communities and a multitude of other communicable diseases, social conflicts and disruptions within communities.

These costs were attributable to a combination of policy and implementation failures that could be addressed through complementary policy and institutional actions. Implementation of those actions could significantly increase the economic, social and environmental benefits of the reform programme. In the mining sector, specific policy and institutional corrections include:

- Revise the mining policy to strengthen the status and opportunities of small-scale miners. This would include providing incentives comparable to those extended to medium- and large-scale mining companies, improving marketing channels and ensuring security of concessions.
- Involve local governments and small-scale miners in the allocation of mining plots. Improve government agency coordination and actively involve communities in issues, such as land tenure, conflict arbitration and resource allocation, which directly affect local communities.
- Enforce mining codes for large- and medium-sized mining companies to reduce environmental damage affecting rural communities,

including requiring all investors to comply with environmental impact assessments.
- Increase the presence of law enforcement agencies to diminish conflicts and abuse of small-scale miners by medium and large companies.
- Enforce revenue collection activities to eliminate rampant corruption.

In the tourism sector, specific policy and institutional corrections should include:

- Develop and adopt a formal tourism act that will translate the tourism policy into a defined set of rights, obligations and standards of behaviour for all agents, large and small, engaged in tourism.
- Exempt tourism from value-added taxation and simplify the current tax structure applied to the sector.
- Establish standards for involving local communities in tourist activities and require mechanisms for revenue-sharing with local communities.
- Apply environmental impact assessments for all tourism enterprises.
- Enforce regulations that are designed to prevent child labour, a common problem in the tourism sector.

Such corrective measures would greatly enhance the long-term contribution of these sectors to the economy and would strengthen community involvement and support.

The Political Realm

The costs of the economic reform programme extend to the political realm as well. Although we have not, in this limited essay, focused on the dynamics of political change in Tanzania, the country's political dynamics have significantly influenced the outcome of the reforms and will continue to influence the beneficiaries and losers of the reforms in coming years. We will note, however, that the failure to establish a transparent and effective regulatory system, and the failure to create conditions in which economic groups and agents can compete fairly, have already generated considerable political costs reflected in the growing public cynicism regarding the emerging economic and political order.

In this regard, although these long-overdue changes in the economic role of the state have engendered an economic dynamism in many sectors, a cloud of mismanagement and corruption hangs over the country's political life. Despite abandoning the one-party regime in 1991, other political parties have not been able to establish deep roots in either urban or rural areas for lack of financial resources and institutional scaffolding. As a consequence, political power remains very much concentrated in a ruling elite still affiliated with the CCM, which has developed an elaborate system of succession and internal control for perpetuating its influence in government. While personalities have changed, cohesive political groups have continued to dominate political and economic decision making. With parliament unable to play an independent oversight role, and with an ineffectual judiciary, the decision-making processes of government remain sheltered from public review and oversight.

This continued centralization of political power in the emerging liberalized economic system has facilitated increasingly close bonds with economic groups whose wealth has increased under the new regime rules. This deepening convergence of political and economic elites has generated widespread malaise about the degree to which corruption dominates national political life. The growing concern about high-level corruption was such that the newly elected President Mkapa set up a commission whose 900-page Warioba report detailed the extent and contours of corruption and proposed reforms for eradicating the growing problem. Despite the release of this report in 1995, the inability of national and international agencies to root out the problem poses serious threats to the viability of government itself, as well as public confidence in the economic system still being put in place.

The situation raises particular alarm for the country's natural resource base since, in Tanzania and elsewhere, these environmental assets have been the direct source of ill-gotten gain and resource rents. Without a transparent regulatory and management system deeply anchored in a functioning public administration, continuation of the corruption and collusion between politicians and private economic agents may well signal further decline and general mismanagement of the country's natural resources. It thus remains to be seen to what degree the new 'political mafia' is able to deepen its hold on the country's diverse and extensive natural resources. In equal measure it remains to be seen if increasingly active groups from civil society, perhaps in conjunction with the international donor community, are able to open the inner workings of government to public scrutiny and hold the political elite accountable for their economic and environmental performance.

A Tentative Balance Sheet

Economic liberalization has brought opportunities to a wide range of economic agents, large and small, national and foreign, operating in Tanzania. Those opportunities are directly attributable to the panoply of economic reforms that dismantled the administered price regime, privatized the marketing system, opened the economy to foreign goods and capital, and established a new set of economic incentives designed to stimulate investment. Natural resource sectors remain at the centre of recent economic growth and will remain central to the country's growth prospects for the foreseeable future. While the long-term benefits for the country's rural poor have yet to materialize for many, both economic and institutional changes have opened opportunities denied to the rural population since independence.

The economic package has been accompanied by multifaceted institutional reforms. Overall, the institutional reforms have sought to deepen the impact of the neoliberal economic regime by creating conditions for private sector investment, reducing the scope of state economic activity and removing institutional constraints on the entrepreneurial activity of corporations and individuals. Since Tanzania's efforts to build agrarian socialism destroyed or displaced traditional tribal leadership in decades past, the recent institutional reforms have not encountered extensive resistance or conflict with traditional leaders on the local level. However, the failure to establish a stable regulatory framework, to ensure the rights of villages to their traditionally-held natural resources, or to provide for mechanisms for enforcing those rights and arbitrating claims, has led to conflicts between villages and the many new economic agents drawn into the countryside as a result of the economic reforms.

The institutional reforms have provided multiple opportunities for companies active in natural resource sectors to take advantage of the weak regulatory framework through tax evasion, corruption and rent-seeking behaviour. Moreover, the central role of natural resource wealth in Tanzania's economy coupled with the lack of political transparency and accountability converge to create extensive corruption and collusion between the economic and political elites. Those institutional problems have weakened public confidence in the country's political system and pose direct, long-term threats to the viability of the country's emerging economy.

These dynamics guarantee that Tanzania will continue to undergo rapid change in coming years. The ability of community-based organizations and other groups of civil society to establish themselves as both watchdogs over government and corporate behaviour and as advocates of reforms promoting public interests will be influential in determining the long-term outcomes of Tanzania's reform process.

ZAMBIA

Chapter 3

Zambia

With Dr Guy Scott[1]

At independence in 1964, Zambia served basically as an unskilled labour reservoir for South Africa and Southern Rhodesia and as a source of abundant, high quality copper and cobalt for the industrialized world. The new nation had minimal manufacturing capacity, woefully inadequate physical and social infrastructure, and limited managerial and intellectual human resources. With this modest inheritance, Zambia faced two principal challenges at the time of its emergence as an independent nation. First, the 1965 proclamation of the Unilateral Declaration of Independence (UDI) by Ian Smith's renegade regime in Southern Rhodesia, now Zimbabwe, created serious security problems along its borders. Second, the boom in copper prices fuelled by the Vietnam War, coupled with the reversion of private mineral royalty rights to the new government, generated unanticipated and abundant revenues for public expenditures. In essence, Zambia was geographically isolated and economically and socially insecure, while also being extremely rich.

---

* Dr Scott is currently director of Mano Consultancy, Inc, based in Lusaka. He served as Minister of Agriculture in the Movement for Multiparty Democracy (MMD) government from 1991 to 1993. He received his PhD from Sussex University and his MA from Cambridge University.

Those economic and political conditions faced the country's ruling party, the United National Independence Party (UNIP), as it tried to forge its own version of African socialism, named 'Humanism', based on state economic and political monopolies. After gaining independence, the government nationalized all sectors of the economy and tried to eliminate political opposition as UNIP extended its institutional scaffolding into all levels of Zambian society. The one-party state also extended its control over Zambia's natural resources, including expansive agricultural lands, broad deposits of mineral and gem ores, abundant wildlife, plentiful groundwater and expanses of woodlands. That resource wealth was to provide the economic foundation on which Zambian socialism was to be constructed.

Within two decades, the economic fortunes of the country changed dramatically. Declining international copper prices and plummeting production levels combined with the more general mismanagement of the statist economy to leave the country one of the poorest and most indebted in the region. Moreover, with loss of superpower sponsors as the Cold War ended in the 1980s, the government could no longer rely on a steady stream of external financing to support its development process. The country was, in short, bankrupt, unable to rekindle growth based on its sunset industry, mining, and had few external supporters willing to overlook the authoritarian political regime. Economic reforms, and political change, were inevitable.

This essay will examine the impact of the economic reform pro-gramme, launched in 1989, on the livelihoods of communities in what are called 'deep rural areas'. The discussion will focus on how the reform programme generated economic dynamics and brought institutional change that provided both new opportunities and new barriers for rural families. Foremost, these changes brought new incentives and manage-ment regimes associated with Zambia's extensive and diverse natural resource wealth. While local studies form the basis of this discussion, we draw links to the broader economic and institutional reforms taking place in the country.

This essay consists of four parts. First, we review the steps taken following independence in 1964 as UNIP established a state-driven economy supported by a one-party political regime. Second, we review how the collapse of the copper-based economy obliged the new government that emerged from a protracted political struggle with UNIP to embark on sweeping economic reforms in 1991. In the third section we review institutional changes that have accompanied the economic reform programme, placing particular emphasis on identifying the impacts on communities in deep rural areas. In the final section we discuss the success and limitations of the reforms in trying to break the structural dualism that has characterized the rural society since the colonial period.

CONSTRUCTING THE AUTHORITARIAN REGIME

Economic and Resource Policy under Kaunda and UNIP

Following a 30-year period as an integral part of Cecil Rhodes' British South Africa Company (BSAC), Northern Rhodesia acquired, in 1924, the status of British Protectorate. While the white and urban population was governed as a colonial administration, areas outside the towns were governed largely through traditional tribal authorities. Relative to Southern Rhodesia, the northern land-locked colony held few attractions for external industrial or agricultural investors. Viewed as the backyard of its southern neighbour, and actually joining in a federation with it from 1952 to 1963, the colony's only attraction was its famous copper industry, concentrated in a small area known as the Copperbelt, which lies close to the Congo border. The colony was essentially an economic enclave for mining companies located in Salisbury (now Harare). Zambia's rural population provided the migrant labour for mining activities in the Copperbelt and in South Africa, and for labour-intensive commercial agriculture in Southern Rhodesia. Profits accumulated in the capitals of its southern neighbours while concession fees and taxes were largely invested in Southern Rhodesia. There were no attempts to bring villagers into Zambia's cash economy as direct producers. Instead various head- and hut-taxes were levied in Zambia to encourage outward migration and integration of the migrant workers into the economies of its neighbours (Henderson 1993; Oliver and Atmore 1967).

The economic policies of the UNIP at independence were fundamentally shaped by this colonial legacy. Foremost among the government's
goals was to break Southern Rhodesia and South Africa's stranglehold
over the fragile economy and its human resources and to render the rural
areas more productive. To this end the government, using copper revenues,
sponsored policies that included:

- positioning non-agricultural investments in rural areas;
- investing in agriprocessing industries;
- establishing state commercial farms and producer cooperatives;
- monopolizing and concentrating commodity marketing; and
- expanding state marketing mechanisms, input provision and a seas-
  onal credit system to deep rural areas.

Cold War alliances with non-aligned countries such as China, Yugoslavia
and Warsaw Pact nations were likewise designed to help secure the
country's economic independence from its stronger southern neighbours. Included in these geopolitical alliances were economic cooperation agreements that led to the construction of the Tazara Railroad to
Dar es Salaam, the highways to Dar es Salaam and provincial capitals,
and hydroelectric plants.

Consistent with UNIP's vision of a non-aligned socialist future, the
president owned natural resources and, acting on behalf of all Zambians,
was empowered to determine how to use that wealth in the development
of the emerging African nation. The most decisive steps in asserting the
state's new authority over natural resources were taken in 1968–69 when
UNIP nationalized all key sectors of the economy, which was heavily
dependent on natural resources. The first institutional pillar by which
the state exerted control over the country's natural resources was the
Zambian Industrial and Mining Corporation (ZIMCO). By 1985,
ZIMCO controlled 121 state companies; the government owned 82 of
them outright, held a majority share in a further 28, and a minority share
in the remaining 11. This gargantuan government holding company was
composed of two basic units including Zambian Consolidated Copper
Mines (ZCCM), which controlled all the mining companies in the
country, and INDECO, the government's industrial holding corpora-

tion. These corporations became the institutions through which a sizeable share of natural resource income was appropriated by the government. Approximately 30 per cent of the country's output was generated through these holding companies (Callaghy 1990).

The second mechanism created by UNIP for managing the country's natural resource wealth was the National Agricultural Marketing Board, or NAMBOARD. This marketing board became the principal mechanism by which the state determined the terms on which rural populations, then 65 per cent of the country's populace, interacted with markets. Through its network of regional cooperatives, the state controlled inputs into agricultural production, notably fertilizer, and set prices on farm produce that was shipped to central marketing and storage centres. This powerful parastatal determined the prices paid for commodities, including maize, terms and levels of credit, and levels of subsidies for fertilizer. The willingness of the NAMBOARD to collect and transport grain from the farthest reaches of the countryside earned UNIP strong support from the peasantry. The monopolistic control exerted over small commodity producers' produce allowed the government to pursue its import substitution industrialization strategy by providing subsidized staples, including maize meal, cooking oil, salt, milk, matches and soap, to urban workers and miners (Bratton 1994).

During the first decade following independence, UNIP was able to live up to its proclaimed motto, 'It pays to belong to UNIP'. This was not an idle boast during the 'fat decade', the first ten years of independence, because the level of capture of resource rents was so steady and so ample that benefits flowed easily from the coffers of the government through its steadily growing network of state employees and rural beneficiaries. One of the remarkable features of statism and authoritarian rule in Zambia in its early years is that it did not rely on overt coercion or naked repression; rather it grew from the delivery of improvements in living standards for the rural population made possible by the transfer of rents from the mining sector to agriculture (Bratton 1994).

Through these institutional arrangements the government was able to centralize the capture of natural resource income drawn from all sectors of the economy. It is important to point out that rents captured by ZIMCO from the copper industry provided resources for Zambia's industrialization programme and supported the extensive subsidies of the agricultural sector. This development approach remained viable only to the degree that the copper industry remained highly profitable and that transfers into the industrial and agricultural sectors generated a steady income flow from its investments. Neither of these conditions held true for long, ultimately precipitating the economic collapse of UNIP's development strategy.

THE IMPERATIVE TO ADJUST

Collapse of the Copper Economy

By 1990 the Zambian economy had collapsed. Investment fell from 24 per cent of GDP in 1986 to barely 9 per cent in 1989. While public and private investment declined, inflation raged out of control, shooting from 35 per cent in 1986 to 154 per cent in 1989. In 1991, copper still accounted for 85 per cent of total exports and about 15 per cent of GDP, despite the fact that the level of copper production actually declined from 700,000 tons to 450,000 tons a year (World Bank 1996b). Internal economic mismanagement and excessive state spending were exacerbated by adverse external conditions, notably the rapidly declining price of copper on international markets and the two oil shocks of the 1970s. As in other oil-importing economies, those exogenous shocks significantly increased the costs of domestic production and disrupted the administered price regime established by the government. Having failed to stimulate steady expansion of either smallholder commodity production or large-scale commercial farming to make up for declining mining revenues, the Zambian economy entered a deep recession.

It is certain that poverty declined during 1960s and early 1970s as Zambians made gains in income, life expectancy, school enrolment and nutrition. These improvements were a central part of UNIP's redistributive policies during the 'fat years' of the 1960s and early 1970s. However, by 1975 those improvements stalled, only to witness steady deterioration thereafter. Per capita GDP fell an average of 2.3 per cent per year during the 1970s and declined another 50 per cent during the decade of the

1980s. By 1990 formal sector incomes had fallen to a mere 25 per cent of their 1975 level. While wage inequalities did narrow between 1975 and 1991, this was due more to a sharp decline at the top of the income scale than to any significant improvements at the low end. By 1991, 67 per cent of Zambians lived in poverty, compared to an estimated 60 per cent in 1975 (World Bank 1996a).

Faced with economic collapse, a team of Zambian economic reformers worked with the World Bank and IMF to design an adjustment programme that would address the most urgent problems besetting the country. The team also hoped that these initial reforms would lay the foundation for liberalizing the statist economy more completely over time. Although President Kaunda reluctantly agreed to implement the reform package in 1985, he found himself surrounded by opponents, both inside and outside the ruling party, who blocked the momentum for reform. Those opponents feared loss of economic benefits, disruption of protected markets and social benefits or, in the case of the labour unions, redundancies in the mines (Callaghy 1990). Support for maintaining the patronage system, albeit an increasingly corrupt one, was so deeply engrained into the country's political economy that the small circle of reformers was unable to mobilize a broader coalition of social groups to support the reform package, regardless of external support from the IMF and World Bank.

Unwilling to recognize the systemic character of the economic collapse, opponents attributed the crisis to external agencies, notably the Bretton Woods institutions, who, they claimed, sought to turn the country back to foreign interests. The efforts to reform proved short-lived as the old guard party elite regained control over the economy, severed ties with the IMF, and declared that the country would articulate its own reform programme and pursue 'growth with our own resources'.

The failure of the cautious, domestically designed reform programme to redress the growing economic problems ultimately reflected the political stalemate in the ruling party and its unwillingness to break decisively with statist economic policies. Resolution of the stalemate came from growing public pressure that was tired of UNIP's corruption and incompetence and wanted fundamental political change. From that opposition movement emerged the Movement for Multiparty

Democracy (MMD) and Frederick Chiluba, the former leader of the Zambian Congress of Trade Unions, later to become the nation's president. That reform movement, however, was grounded in the trade union movement which made itself accountable to urban groups and organizations in which political mobilization and recruitment proved easiest. That urban bias would prevail throughout the MMD's political reign during the subsequent decade (Bratton and van der Walle 1992).

When the MMD took power in November 1991, its team of economic reformers quickly set about charting the restructuring of the Zambian economy with guidance from the Bretton Woods institutions. Three central pillars constituted the country's economic reform package:

1   Opening the economy to foreign markets and investors. Reforms have included providing incentives to attract foreign investors, removing all controls on foreign currency exchange (one of two countries in Africa without controls), and reducing tariffs and export controls. The government has also employed strict fiscal controls to dampen inflation and reduce budget deficits.
2   Reducing the economic role of the state. Foremost, reforms have sought and, to a large extent, have succeeded in privatizing para-statals, divesting state-owned farms and marketing boards, and selling off government monopolies. Reforms have also improved management of public utilities and, to a certain degree, reformed the civil service (although, contrary to MMD promises, the civil service actually grew by 19 per cent between 1989 and 1994 (Rakner et al 1999)). Reforms also sought to strengthen social safety nets through targeted social welfare programmes and public works projects.
3   Reforming and diversifying the agricultural sector. Reforms have sought to establish a market-based pricing regime, reduce distortionary effects of government subsidies, and encourage national and foreign investors to diversify agricultural production and expand agricultural processing industries (World Bank 1996b).

The Reform Package

During the ensuing decade, the MMD remained committed to both stabilization policies agreed with the IMF and structural reforms undertaken with the World Bank to liberalize the economy. That commitment, at least in principle, has thus far ensured a flow of external financial support. A key element of the reform package was the government's determination to implement a cash budget by 1993, to which the government has adhered despite adverse external economic and internal financial conditions. A tangible result of that fiscal discipline has been the lowering of inflation rates from around 200 per cent in 1993 to 40 per cent or less in the late 1990s. By 1999, more than 80 per cent of state enterprises had been privatized, with major exceptions including the state mining company (ZCCM), the railways, the electricity utility (ZESCO), and the postal and telecommunications services. Although final revenues from divestiture have proven far lower than anticipated, government deficits have improved, as highly subsidized industries have been off-loaded. National value-added taxes and a more efficient tax collection system have helped stabilize the revenue side of government accounts (Rakner et al 1999).

Reforming the agricultural sector was given high priority by the team of reformers in the early 1990s. That priority was obvious since future national economic development was tied to increasing non-traditional agricultural exports to offset the anticipated decline in mining revenues (World Bank 1996a). Market liberalization and privatization of production and marketing systems have allowed large agricultural operations to expand and improve efficiency. For example, the Zambia Sugar Company expanded considerably, and Lonrho Cotton – once operating in the shadow of the government-controlled Lintco – purchased the parastatal in 1994 and has since become the largest cotton grower in the country. Similarly, the Tobacco Association of Zambia took over the moribund state-owned tobacco factory, turning the enterprise into a profit-generating company. Liberalization of export markets and removal of price controls has allowed Zambian producers to sell at higher prices and has encouraged export of non-traditional agricultural products such as flowers, paprika and guar beans. In 1994, the value of all non-traditional exports was approximately US$38 million; in 1998 the value was more than US$110 million, an increase of almost 200 per cent.

Perhaps most successful of the large-scale agribusiness investments was the Mpongwe Development Company, which managed large irrigated farms producing wheat, maize, soya and coffee in the Copperbelt Province. The Masstock farm, the Lonrho cotton outgrower scheme, the Banana Scheme and Kateshi Coffee Estate, having benefited from high levels of initial government subsidies, created employment opportunities and increased food security in deep rural areas. Numerous community-based investment programmes, supported directly by foreign donors, proved more vulnerable and less profitable in rural Zambia.

Paradoxically, while foreign investment increased during this period, maize production dropped nearly 40 per cent and Zambia found itself moving from relative food self-sufficiency to an expected food deficit. Strict monetary policy has created a credit squeeze that has pushed many small-scale commercial farmers out of business, hence increasing the risk that Zambia will need to import basic foodstuffs to support its population. The removal of fertilizer subsidies, by which poor farmers were able to increase production, has led to extensification of the agricultural frontier and a return to slash and burn techniques with attendant environmental consequences.

As regards the mining sector, no area has generated more friction between government agencies and the Bretton Woods institutions as privatization of ZIMCO and ZCCM. The issue of privatization first found its way onto the agenda of the World Bank's Consultative Group meetings in December 1993 and steadily rose on the list of priority negotiation points with the government. During the eight years before the state mining corporation was finally privatized, production plummeted, investment stagnated, infrastructure deteriorated and environmental externalities increased at the same time that tens of thousands of miners were laid off. Only extraordinary external pressure, taking the form of withholding balance of payments support in 1997 and 1998, finally convinced the government to sell ZCCM. The company was sold to Anglo-America Corporation in 1999, at a price far below its potential sale price several years earlier (Economist Intelligence Unit 2000).

Despite improvement of a few traditional economic indicators, the formal economy has continued its steady decline, including a 4 per cent annual decline in per capita income since the mid-1970s (Rakner et al 1999). While reforms have succeeded in improving the fiscal balance, the continued economic decline and debt overhang have squeezed public expenditures. Even with improvements in economic growth, the debt-to-GDP ratio has remained high, which has left little room for social, infrastructure, agriculture or environmental spending. Although the government made progress in reducing subsidies, government-controlled companies are still heavily subsidized. Moreover, employment in the formal sector dropped more than 50 per cent during the 1990s due to the loss of civil service and industrial jobs.

---

45 per cent of Zambians live in absolute poverty.
69 per cent of rural Zambians live in absolute poverty (as against 27 per cent of urban dwellers).
85 per cent of Zambians earn less than US$1 per day (the second highest percentage worldwide).
98 per cent of Zambians earn less than US$2 per day.
47 per cent of Zambians do not reach their 40th birthday (the 4th highest percentage worldwide)

INSTITUTIONAL REFORMS FOR RURAL COMMUNITIES

Structural Dualism

The government of Zambia and international agencies have long since agreed that shifting the country from a copper economy to one based on export of non-traditional agricultural products is the key to ensuring the country's economic stability and growth. Beyond that general orientation, however, reforms in the sector have been characterized by frequently changing priorities and policies. Admittedly, adverse external conditions, including the collapse of copper prices and drought, contributed to the policy swings. Those external conditions notwithstanding, agricultural policy has been marked by changes in subsidy, credit and marketing policies, among others, creating inconsistency and uncertainties for large and small producers.

There has been, however, a unifying thread in policies to reform the agricultural sector: trying to 'break the dualistic structure' of Zambian agriculture. By dualism we mean the coexistence of commercial agriculture producing market goods with hired labour and peasants who produce non-tradables and petty commodities on the basis of family labour, while occasionally providing cheap labour to the commercial sector (de Janvry 1981). One can safely assume that the objective of ending dualism in the Zambian context implies integrating the peasant producer more directly into the money economy by: transforming subsistence farming into market production, increasing wage-labour on commercial farms, diversifying production on-farm and expanding off-farm activities, and a host of other economic pursuits by which the peasant is directly integrated into the formal economy. The following quote from the World Bank publication, *Prospects for Sustainable Growth* (1996b) reflects that thrust:

> It is vital that Zambia's pattern of growth be increasingly inclusive, breaking unequivocally from the country's long-standing economic dualism. An increasingly inclusive pattern of growth would be rural-oriented, with strong emphasis on participation by emergent and smallholder farmers.

That orientation underlies not only the economic policies driving sectoral reform but also captures the rationale for institutional reforms that the government and international agencies have pursued to promote agricultural growth. One can hardly take issue with the priority placed on promoting increased participation by emergent and smallholder farmers. However, while the institutional vehicles for pursuing that objective have generated opportunities for some, the outcomes have proven disruptive and destabilizing for many rural poor.

UNIP's Institutional Grip

To understand those outcomes we need to review, albeit in general terms, the development of rural institutions in Zambia. Of all the countries of colonial southern Africa, the traditional tribal governance system in Zambia remained most firmly intact up to and beyond independence. Rural areas held little interest for largely urban British colonists of Northern Rhodesia except as an abundant source of cheap domestic labour and workers for copper mines. In stark contrast to the settler plantations in neighbouring Southern Rhodesia and Tanganyika, few large agricultural companies claimed or cultivated the extensive and fertile soils of the land-locked colony. As a consequence, two largely separate forms of land and resource tenure existed side-by-side for decades with comparatively little interaction.

With independence and UNIP's commitment to opening development opportunities for rural Zambians, institutional arrangements underwent significant change. When the government created NAMBOARD, it also implemented a nationwide land reform measure in 1975 known as the *Conversion of Titles Act*. This law abolished freehold land titles and gave ownership of all land to the president who, as the principal landholder, granted rights and interests to individuals through two forms of ownership. The first, covering approximately 90 per cent of all lands, concerns lands held under the traditional land tenure system; the second, under statutory tenure, covers the remaining parcels. The intent of this act was to facilitate the conversion of traditional to statutory tenure, with the state as landlord. Given the predominance of traditional or customary tenure, this Act recognized the influence that chieftains or village headmen played in determining use and allocation of land. Under this arrangement, the land was considered to belong to the community as a whole and use thereof was determined by rules established on the communal level (Kambenja 1996; Mano 2000).

The state's intent to establish presidential control of the land had a parallel in the wildlife sector. When UNIP took power in 1964 it set out to erode the limited control and revenue-sharing arrangements with local communities established during the colonial period. This intent was reflected in UNIP's decree that all tourism revenues were to be retained by the central government. Having gained centralized control, the government encouraged commercial hunting in order to generate maximum revenues from game hunting, but had no integrated wildlife management plan. On the village level, local chiefs, having lost their previous stake in sustainable wildlife management, supported the bur- geoning world market for ivory and rhino horn by actively encouraging poaching. Their direct deals with safari operators left a modicum of revenues in the villages in contrast to the government's approach that left only burdens and no revenue. The rapid disappearance of Zambian wildlife during the first 15 years following independence finally led the government to establish various community-based natural resource management systems, including the ADMADE programme, to increase local management and revenue sharing. Despite the apparent reversal in policy, local rights and opportunities were consistently undermined by the central government as it continued to issue special hunting licences to friends and clients.

Perhaps as significant as implementing these resource management reforms, UNIP opened political offices in rural communities and urban areas across the country. These offices were responsible for overseeing local councils, ensuring compliance with decrees passed by the central government and controlling political activities. Within a short time, these offices created conflicts with local authorities whose decision- making processes were based on customary laws and governance pro- cesses. Given, however, the extensive patronage system and the ruling party's ability to provide resources for local projects during the ten years following independence, political officers carried considerable sway over local decision-making and resource distribution.

As the copper-based economy collapsed and discontent rose in equal measure during the late 1980s, political strife between UNIP and the emerging MMD increased in rural areas. Given the relative newness and weak institutional scaffolding of the MMD, UNIP's grip on the country- side remained strong, while the MMD drew its supporters from urban areas and the miners' union. Even with the victory of the MMD in November 1991, UNIP offices continued to have influence over local economic and political life in rural areas (Burnell 1999).

The MMD's Turn

As the new government worked with the World Bank and international agencies to implement structural reforms, they also set about designing institutional changes that could support the economic programmes. Given the centrality of reforming the agricultural sector, land reform became the institutional centrepiece, taking form in the *Lands Act* of 1995. Donors and government alike viewed the Act as the pivotal piece in increasing productivity in the agricultural sector. In essence, the Act sought to establish landholdings as an asset with cash value that could facilitate investment and credit making in the moribund sector. This valuation or monetization of land sought, among other objectives, to transfer customary or traditional tenure to leasehold tenure – that is, leasehold title granted by the president for 99 years. From the time of its promulgation, confusion reigned regarding the rights and mechanisms by which local communities and individuals could obtain title to lands under their control in years prior. This uncertainty has generated a steadily growing number of claims arising from customary users and chieftains seeking to protect their access to land from new claimants, both national and foreign (Mano 2000; Kambenja 1997).

Parallel to the *Lands Act* of 1995, the MMD government, pressured steadily by the donor community, implemented a series of reforms to alter management of wildlife and forestry, two key areas affecting rural livelihoods. The *Wildlife Act* of 1998, actively promoted by the European Union, grew from the continual management problems and lack of resources affecting the National Parks and Wildlife Service. In creating the Zambian Wildlife Authority (ZAWA) through the *Wildlife Act*, government and donors sought to create an independent authority that would be financially self-sustaining while generating higher revenues for the tourism sector. Under the Act, ZAWA is to be financed from local tourism revenues, a measure that eases the financial burden on government budgets. That new appropriation of wildlife rents diminishes the revenues made available to local tribes and communities, the custodians of wildlife. An important feature of the Act is the removal of tribal chiefs as chairpersons of the community-based natural resource management committees, local boards which oversee tourism activities and are used to provide resources for community improvement activities.

More recently, the *Forestry Act* of 1999, following the model set by the ZAWA, has sought to establish the Zambian Forestry Commission with the primary goal of increasing the national revenues from the forestry sector. While the wildlife authority has to address established relationships of management and revenue sharing with local chiefs, the Forestry Commission faces no such prior restraints. As a consequence, it is intended that the revenues for the Commission are captured by the Commission itself to fund staff and other investments while little, if any, resource rents are distributed to local communities whose forested lands are being harvested.

Impact of Reforms on Deep Rural Areas

The studies of two deep rural areas, Chiawa and Kaindu, provided insights into the impacts of economic liberalization and institutional reforms on rural livelihoods. These two areas are representative of conditions in many parts of rural Zambia in that subsistence agriculture plays a central role in livelihoods at the same time that villagers engage in other economic activities such as tourism and agricultural wage labour to sustain their families. Chiawa is the most remote part of Lusaka Province, lying on the floodplain of the Zambezi River contiguous with the Chiawa Game Management Area. Chiawa is notable because of the important role that tourism plays, or could potentially play, in community members' wellbeing. Kaindu is an important example because of the role played by a cotton outgrower scheme sponsored by Lonrho Cotton, the country's largest cotton producer, in generating local income. This area, comparatively rich in natural resources, lies just east of the Kafue National Park.

Livelihoods in Chiawa have been influenced by macroeconomic policy changes including removal of exchange rate controls, lifting of price controls on basic commodities, revision of the *Lands Act*, and a general relaxation of the regulatory environment. These reforms have been felt most directly in the tourism sector, where liberalization has clearly stimulated an increase in tourism, mostly by people from South Africa and Europe. Perhaps the most noticeable change has been the increase in foreign tour operators in the area, who have expanded the frequency of short-term safaris and rafting tours in the river basin. Local tour operators have not responded to the new economic regime because tight monetary policy has made obtaining loans for investment difficult and because the new tax system places an additional burden on local companies.

Foreign tour operators have, in effect, established small enclaves in the Chiawa area that generate very limited economic opportunities for local villagers. Regular and part-time employees are seldom hired from the community; operators import food and water, and build lodgings with imported materials. Conflicts between villagers and tour operators have escalated in recent years as the ability of the local chieftainess to control construction, safaris and other tourist activities has become increasingly uncertain. Without clear regulatory guidelines and administrative control, granting of permits, payment of royalty fees, contracting of local workers, compensation for damages, payment for managing wildlife and other services remain beyond the control of local authorities. That said, there have been economic spin-offs benefiting the region. Tour operators have occasionally purchased thatching mats and local produce, and hired short-term labourers, thereby increasing local incomes albeit in nominal ways.

The economic reforms have been felt in other ways as well in the communities. On the beneficial side, deregulation of prices and marketing arrangements has spawned a number of small-scale kiosks, increased commerce of basic necessities, opened markets and diversified production of local produce, stimulated micro-enterprises for goods and services, and improved access to transport. These represent tangible improvements in the livelihoods of many villagers.

There are also significant and tangible economic costs associated with the new economic dynamism. Foremost among them is the increased conflict between rural communities and wildlife, including elephants and hippos, which are protected under wildlife management arrangements. A growing number of incidences of destruction of crops and homes and of physical injury is part of the record of the increase in tourism and wildlife ranching. In addition, conflicts between villagers and tourists and tour operators are increasing in frequency and intensity as the tourist parties increase contacts and place further demands on local natural resources.

The negative impacts, however, have come primarily through changing institutional conditions. Foremost among those problems is the growing sense of lack of control and uncertainty about land and natural resource use. Control by the chieftainess, the traditional authority, over farming and fishing rights is not only uncertain but has generated rulings which compete with national agencies such as the National Parks and Wildlife Service and with Kafue District Council. Moreover, new economic agents, often connected and supported by national-level sponsors, have attempted to take control of game management lands and to establish their authority over tourism, agriculture and extractive activities in areas under traditional authority. Similar efforts to take over lands have been sponsored by international development agencies, often acting through local and international non-governmental organizations. If there has been one positive institutional change, it is the disappearance of UNIP and its local representatives as other political parties have increased their visibility.

The situation in Kaindu is equally instructive. To begin, a historical footnote. In the 1950s a large estate, the Big Concession, was converted to state land with a view to settlement by white settler farmers. However, the poor infrastructure and lack of surface water discouraged investment, leaving the concession designated as 'titled bush' owned mostly by absentee Zambian landlords who lack the resources to develop it. Local inhabitants cannot develop the land. In the 1980s, a comparable experience further weakened the economic opportunities of the community. At that time, the Kaluanyembe area (Kaindu), a huge area adjacent to the Kafue National Park, was slated to be classified as a game management area. This would have entitled the area to special rights and income under a national resource management programme called ADMADE. The area even appeared on national maps, indicating that the area was to acquire special status. However, due to the mysterious workings of national authorities, the new classification was not completed and, instead, the two-stage process of converting the area to private ownership adjacent to the Kafue National Park took place instead. At this time not enough unclaimed land remains in the area to support a viable ADMADE programme which could support a significant rise in community incomes through tourism. Tension and hostility remain between the community, whose lands were taken, and the present owners, who are promoting a game ranching enterprise.

Today, the main source of cash income is an outgrower scheme of Lonrho Cotton. Of its over 100,000 small contract growers nationwide, Lonrho holds similar contracts with 323 producers in Kaindu. This contractual relationship is a direct byproduct of the liberalization reforms of the 1990s. Small growers have enjoyed some economic benefits from the outgrower scheme but the continued existence of the programme is very much uncertain as global cotton prices continue to fall. Given the limited rainfall, the area holds little potential for production of other commodities.

There are a number of potential small-scale non-agricultural opportunities in the area. Fishing is practised on the Kafue at an artisanal level. The fishermen are largely migrants and itinerant fishermen who move from one depleted fishery to a new one. The area has no big fishing operations, and the potential for expanding the fishing industry is limited. Mining is showing potential for economic development. There are some small-scale mining operations managed by illegal and part-time village miners. In addition, there is interest in prospecting for gold, silver and copper in the area, but actual exploitation is limited due to poor infrastructure.

The recent development of commercial game ranching and the declining influence of traditional and elected community leadership is particularly instructive regarding the opportunities and obstacles now facing rural communities under the liberalized economic regime and its accompanying institutional arrangements. Mumbwa District Council acquired permission from the former Chief Kaindu to covert 56,000 hectares of land in the area for game ranching as a means of generating council income. The council then decided not to proceed with the project and did not acquire the title to the land. By means unknown and without the approval of the previous or current Chief Kaindu, the land was instead demarcated into six farms ranging from 4000 hectares to

15,000 hectares and allocated to individual applicants and companies. At present, the new owners are threatening villagers with eviction from the river frontage since their claims apparently override all community water and other communal rights and render the community helpless and vulnerable. As a result, villagers have become trespassers and do not know how to approach the Lands Tribunal or High Court for litigation; nor can they afford legal action.

Opportunities and Growing Conflicts

The experiences of these two cases are replicated with variations in rural areas across the country, reflecting both the new opportunities and the growing conflicts taking form in rural Zambia.

On the local level, tour operators, largely foreign, have benefited from the liberalization of the economy through increased access to natural resources, wildlife, rivers and the resources of local communities when they are needed. Commercial farmers and game ranchers have taken advantage of the *Lands Act* to acquire control of vast stretches of land; they have also benefited from new investment incentives that open opportunities to convert community-controlled land into private reserves for tourism. Agribusiness has also benefited from the removal of constraints on its activities, lifting of price controls, change in land tenure, and the government's willingness to grant ownership to expanses of land previously held under traditional control.

While consolidation of the neoliberal land tenure regime is far from complete, the path has been cleared to expand the presence of medium and large commercial farming throughout the country's fertile lands. In this context, agribusiness stands to benefit from the institutional reforms for years to come. Though not summarized above, we should point out that expansion of agribusiness has brought significant environmental damage to Zambia's surface water through fertilizer concentrations, livestock waste and discharge from processing plants. Given the virtually non-existent capacity of the government to regulate these environmental problems, commercial farmers and agribusiness have little concern about the environmental costs of their growing operations.

The status and future of local communities and small farmers is an entirely different story. The *Lands Act* of 1995 has significantly weakened the status and decision-making power of traditional authorities, including the House of Chiefs, individual chiefs and district administrators. Under the new tenure regime, their ability to designate users of communal resources and to provide a communal management service to the local population has decreased. Moreover, local inhabitants have incurred other losses through:

- increased crop damage and risk to life caused by wild animals;
- reduced protein availability from subsistence hunting;
- reduced access to fishing as a livelihood; and
- increased dependency ratios, partly due to the emigration of income earners.

Similar outcomes are foreseen for the economic and institutional reforms being implemented for other natural resource sectors, such as forestry. The Forest Commission, created and endowed with broad authority under the *Forestry Act* of 1999, will have access to forested lands that once fell under the control of local authorities. Under this new arrangement the government will stand to benefit, on one hand, by cleansing its budget of employees and, on the other, through access to resource rents from the forests, a sector that remained largely unexploited in previous decades. Private forest corporations will likewise stand to gain under the reforms from contracts and leases to operate in previously restricted areas, and from new access to domestic and international markets.

If patterns of the recent past are replicated in the forestry sector, local communities, who previously managed forests, will stand to lose. Despite assertions that the Act is designed to increase the opportunities and participation of local communities, the role of communities is very uncertain, particularly as regards their usufruct rights. Moreover, given the emphasis of the Commission on increasing revenues from the sector, doubts reign over the ability of the communities to manage timber plantations in a profitable yet sustainable manner without steady technical input from government agencies or private companies, input that can seldom be counted on.

DISMANTLING DUALISM: TO WHOSE BENEFIT?

If the path traced by the current economic and institutional reforms continues, there is little doubt that structural dualism in Zambia will undergo significant change. The questions raised by the local examples sketched above are: what kind of change is really taking place under the reform programme, and whose interests are those changes serving? In answering those questions, we should recognize that two distinct readings of the experiences presented above are feasible. For example, one can view the changes as creating better conditions in which a market-based economy can flourish. The outcome of those changes will include creating employment possibilities, diversifying incomes, drawing the peasants into national economic life and thereby opening economic and social prospects previously beyond reach. The institutional reforms, in that perspective, provide the mechanisms by which those new economic opportunities become available to the rural communities.

In contrast, one can view the economic reforms as providing the opportunity for the wealthier sectors of Zambian society and foreign companies to pry natural resources away from the peasants. The economic and institutional reforms allow companies and individuals based largely in the nation's capital to apply new statutes, regulatory standards and political arrangements to land, forests, water, and wildlife and fishery resources and assert legal control where they once had none. Those changes can be interpreted essentially as the machinations of politicians and their cronies, which peasants can neither influence nor resist.

Unquestionably there is an element of truth in both of these perspectives. Some rural families are enjoying new economic opportunities and gaining access to material goods that were far beyond their grasp a decade ago. By the same token, many families and communities are losing control over their resources, and losing authority and economic opportunity through displacement and dispossession. It is also certain that the economic reforms are largely irreversible at this time and that institutional reform will continue to accompany their implementation in coming years. It is equally clear, however, that simply continuing to push policy and institutional reforms in the current direction will continue to deepen conflicts in rural areas, with the poor, vulnerable communities most likely to experience the highest costs.

The prescribed economic and institutional changes are not, however, immutable. Significant alterations can be made to protect the interests of the rural communities without undermining those reforms essential to dismantling the statist economy. Below, we have listed some of the basic and urgent changes whose implementation could significantly improve the outcomes of the reform process for rural communities.

First and foremost is revising the *Lands Act* of 1995. The Act targets foreign and national investors as the primary beneficiaries, often to the exclusion or detriment of the rural poor. Implementation failures and ineffective administration have distorted the impact of the Act so that it is used with impunity by powerful economic corporations and individuals to gain control over communal lands. Not surprisingly, this Act was implemented under steady pressure from international agencies despite widespread expressions of concern that major problems were imbedded in its provisions. Changes should include:

- revise the Act to empower customary land tenure holders to gain access to credit financing;
- recognize customary land rights in rural areas and guarantee customary holders non-displacement;
- ensure that community land rights are protected to avoid litigation, or provide assistance to local communities in litigation cases; and
- translate the main provisions of the Act into local languages to enable the people to understand their legal rights.

Second, even though the government faces serious resource constraints at the national level, there are many simple changes in policy application that would be highly beneficial for rural communities from economic, social and environmental perspectives. These changes are, in the main, concerned with the implementation of policies to which the government and development organizations officially are committed but which they seldom respect. They must:

- increase fiscal authority on a local level;
- strengthen local control over natural resources; and
- enhance and rationalize local managerial capacity.

Towards a New Authoritarianism?

Owing in large part to the acute dependence of the government on external funding, it has religiously respected certain aspects of the reform process, notably complying with cash budget restrictions. However, that determined compliance has made the lack of a broader development strategy stand out in stark relief. As one analyst noted,

> Both the Zambian government and the donors have failed to express a coherent strategy of economic growth. Instead, both the government and the donors have made fiscal austerity an end in itself and a measure of reform commitment (Rakner et al 1999).

Without an internal consensus on a future development strategy, without a workable vision of the role, status, and character of rural Zambia, and without a government accountable to the public, the Bretton Woods institutions have used the tenets of the Washington consensus to drive the country's development policy with its attendant costs and benefits.

During the past 15 years, Zambian politicians have vacillated between mobilizing public opinion in opposition to adjustment, ignoring agreed upon reforms through inaction, and fervently embracing elements of structural change. Amid these changing orientations, resistance to economic liberalization and privatization was never greater than in ceding control of the country's ample natural resource wealth to the private sector. Relinquishing direct control over mineral wealth, forests, wildlife and land represented a mortal blow to both the nationalist ideology and the statist economic system based on rent seeking and monopoly.

Despite the policy swings and resistance, structural changes have brought irrevocable change to Zambian society. The old one-party elite of UNIP has been unceremoniously displaced by the MMD, its statist economy turned over to private companies and, for a brief moment, hopes of democratic governance seemed to take hold. The protracted process of privatizing natural resource wealth and liberalizing the economy has slowly created conditions conducive to dismantling the authoritarian structures and clientelism kept in place in various forms over the past 40 years.

During the past decade, however, a new political elite associated with the economic reform programme has become entrenched at the centre of the government. This elite, positioned at the crossroads of the country's economic and political life, has actively pursued new forms of collusion and corruption that bind the new and emerging economic agents from the private sector to its political control. There is, in short, a consolidation of power in a small coterie of political and economic interests whose actions and decisions rest far from the light of public scrutiny.

The consolidation of the new political and economic elite poses particular threats to the future wellbeing of the rural population. As pointed out above, the institutional reforms being implemented already pose serious threats to the influence and stability of community-level organizations and authorities. Their impact is exacerbated by the government's decentralization strategy, which promises to increase the benefits accruing to communities but which, in reality, has meant relinquishing control over revenues and resources to the central government. Through these changes, the authority and power of villages and chiefs over natural resources, be it land, water, wildlife or forests, have steadily eroded, and the ability of individual users to gain title or effective control is increasingly uncertain. Communities often seem to be at the mercy of forces that they can neither name nor influence.

A Tentative Balance Sheet

This review of the reform experience draws into focus the efforts to promote desperately needed structural changes through an essentially predetermined reform package that was poorly adapted to the Zambian context. The overall goals of reducing the economic preponderance of the state, increasing the role of the private sector, providing incentives to diversify and expand the agricultural sector and reestablishing the fiscal balance were basic requisites for putting Zambia on a sustained growth path. Continued resistance from the political elite rendered implementing those reforms a daunting task for the better part of a decade. That those fundamental reforms have taken root holds promise for building a more dynamic, responsive economic system in the future.

Despite those gains, what remains particularly disturbing about the Zambian experience is the gross disregard that designers of the reform package, largely external experts associated with the Bretton Woods institutions, showed for the political and institutional arrangements that shaped Zambian life. That disregard began with the failure to understand the structure and exercise of power on the national level and the economic foundations, ie natural resource wealth, on which that power rested. Repeated flip-flops in embracing or repudiating authoritarian rulers, disregard and exclusion of civil society, and ignoring of the role of clientelism in knitting Zambian society together in the post-independence period, are reflections of that dismissive approach.

Most disturbing in this regard, however, is the insistence of external agencies on imposing institutional reforms that have generated conflicts among political elites, rural communities and traditional authorities. External agencies, ranging from the Bretton Woods institutions to the European Union and bilateral agencies, have financed institutional reforms that are allegedly designed to deepen market reforms and increase aggregate economic productivity but which, in reality, are more appropriate for northern societies sponsoring the changes. Those institutional changes remain among the most controversial features of the Zambian reform process because they have pitted the least powerful social groups, including rural farmers and rural communities, against the most powerful, politically adept groups in the country as well as against foreign corporations.

Equally disturbing is the process by which economic reforms and institutional changes have created a new political and economic elite whose actions and policies lie beyond the realm of public scrutiny and accountability. While, on the one hand, the Bretton Woods institutions promote strictures of good governance and disseminate prescriptions for combating corruption, the fact remains that the economic reform process it sponsored played a fundamental role in consolidating the new elite that holds the reins of economic and political power much to the detriment of broad sectors of Zambian society.

Amid the changing mosaic of Zambian economic and political life, the rural population, despite gains by some individuals and communities, seems to have lost the most and seems destined to continue experiencing loss in the future. This conclusion is paradoxical because the expressed purpose of the economic reforms, as articulated by the Bretton Woods institutions over the past decade, has been to alleviate poverty, particularly rural poverty, and to draw the peasantry fully into the country's economic life.

What is certain is that the economic and institutional reforms have again placed the struggle over natural resource wealth at the centre of the country's development process. Today, the deepening collusion between the political elite and private sector interests creates a formidable alliance that is determined to increase its control over the country's natural resources. That alliance can count as well on multinational corporations equally interested in expanding their access to Zambia's natural resource wealth. In that context, villagers and traditional authorities will face a dogged struggle to assert their rights and establish their rightful place in the future development of the country.

ZIMBABWE

Chapter 4

Zimbabwe

In 1889, the British Crown granted Cecil Rhodes the right to establish a chartered company, the British South Africa Company (BSAC), in the area covered by Northern and Southern Rhodesia. Driven by the hope that the reported gold fields in the area would turn into a 'second Rand' (referring to the extensive reef gold deposits found in the Witwatersrand of South Africa in 1886), Rhodes invested considerable resources in constructing rail lines and other infrastructure in the region. When his mining enterprise in Southern Rhodesia failed in a few short years, Rhodes then tried to recoup investment losses by attracting British settlers to expand agricultural production on the fertile lands of his sprawling territory. Since that time, the political economy of the region has been shaped by conflicts between white settlers and the native African population in their efforts to control the productive lands of the area.

The successful struggle for nationhood in 1980 and the rise to political dominance of the Zimbabwe African National Union Patriotic Front (ZANU-PF) did not attenuate the conflict over who was to control the new country's land and natural resources. The decades-old tensions between white settlers and African villagers were transferred to the political dynamics of an independent country, where they took the form of balancing two contradictory forces. On the one hand the new government sought to protect the economic structure dominated by the whites and, on the other, it sought to establish a political monopoly to govern the country. As one political analyst commented:

> [At independence] the Government adopted a two-pronged political manifesto: reconciliation and national unity. In practice the former meant the toleration of continued white control of the economy, and the latter came to mean one-party rule *(Jenkins 1997)*.

Although it has required 20 years, growing inequalities, abject poverty and environmental degradation in rural areas affecting millions of Africans has shattered the illusion that fundamental change in that arrangement can be avoided.

The implementation of structural reforms launched in 1990 grew not from financial or structural crisis but rather from the needs of the white industrial sector to open the country to international markets. Ten years following independence, growth of Zimbabwean industry and commercial agriculture depended on accessing new markets, acquiring new technology and capital, and putting the economy on a more competitive foundation. However, clearly absent from that impetus to reform the economy was any intent to alter the basic relations of natural resource ownership and, least of all, to bring fundamental change to land tenure relations between white commercial farmers and Africans living in communal areas.

As the economic reforms took hold in the 1990s, tourism experienced a significant and sustained expansion, unexpectedly raising this natural resource-intensive sector to the fourth largest component of the Zimbabwean economy. Even as the rest of the economy contracted or stagnated in subsequent years, tourism continued to create new employment and generate revenues for the government. One of the key questions that needed attention in that growth process, however, was how to ensure that the economic benefits associated with the growth of tourism would accrue to millions of poor Africans who scratched out livings in the degraded, comparatively unproductive lands of the communal areas. What economic opportunities were to be accorded to the guardians of Zimbabwe's wildlife at the local level and under what conditions could the benefits flowing to the rural poor increase?

As we sought answers to those questions, however, it became apparent that any significant change regarding beneficiaries of the tourist sector expansion would ultimately be linked to the land question. Improving the incomes going to African villages from tourism depended on changing the terms of access to land and increasing the control of villagers over productive soils, wildlife and other natural resources. Sam Moyo, Zimbabwe's most articulate analyst and advocate of land reform, commented that 'land is a political good', a good used for political ends and not necessarily accorded its proper status as the linchpin for promoting sustainable development in the country (Moyo 1991). In short, increasing returns to the poor African villages from tourism, a natural resource-intensive sector, would be resolved on the political level and would be intimately tied to resolution of the growing tensions over land.

In the first section of this chapter, we briefly summarize the patterns and relations of natural resource management established by the settler regime during the colonial period including the UDI (Unilateral Declaration of Independence) lasting from 1965 until 1980, when the Lancaster House Agreement established the terms of Zimbabwe's independence. The second section covers the post-independence regime, including the period from 1990 onward during which time the government implemented a structural adjustment programme. In the context of the structural reforms, we share the results of several studies of the local impacts of tourism expansion. To help interpret the different effects of tourist growth on the rural poor, we drew extensively on the work of Sam Moyo in analysing how structural reforms altered land uses and land markets in ways that ultimately deepened the racially defined class structure of Zimbabwean society.

THE FOUNDATIONS OF CONFLICT

Settler Colonialism

In 1889, the British Crown granted the BSAC a 25-year charter to manage the territory known as Southern Rhodesia. During the following seven years, the BSAC granted 16 million acres, or one-sixth of the entire territory, to white immigrants in the form of large-scale land concessions. By 1913, one year before the BSAC's charter came up for renewal, 21.5 million acres had been accorded to white settlers (Mosley 1983). In addition, cash transactions, often forced, between Africans and arriving settlers expanded the landholdings of the whites so rapidly in the early 1900s that the very survival of rural Africans seemed at risk.

By encouraging European immigration and settlement in his Crown-granted monopoly, however, Cecil Rhodes sowed the seeds of his own demise as an increasingly productive and unified group of commercial farmers ceased to accept his autocratic control. On the fertile lands of Southern Rhodesia, white settlers produced a diverse array of agricultural commodities destined for domestic, South African and international markets and expanded activities of both small and large-scale mining enterprises. The growing wealth and economic dynamism of the settler colony, as well as their need to implement beneficial economic and administrative policies, generated more frequent conflict with the BSAC. The contention with BSAC over land, railway fees and economic policy rose to the point that, in 1923, the British government granted increased autonomy so that Southern Rhodesia became, to all intents and purposes, a self-governing settler colony (Skälnes 1995).

As the economic opportunities for the settlers increased, conflicts with African farmers likewise intensified as both economic groups competed for land and markets. Through its control of the economy and political mechanisms, the settler community imposed a series of restrictive measures on African farmers that were ultimately codified in the *Land Apportionment Act* of 1930. That decree established the principle that 'land which was already occupied by Europeans, or which might in the future be required for European settlement, was not set aside as African reserve' (Mosley 1983). In this manner two separate 'non-markets' were established, ensuring that Africans could not penetrate or buy their way into the formal European land markets. Africans were allocated 7.4 million acres of 'native purchase areas' wherein they could exchange and purchase property assigned to them. In addition, differential prices were set for African produce and taxes were imposed on villagers, among other measures, to place African farmers at severe economic disadvantage (Skälnes 1995).

One of the most important measures taken to regulate control of the country's natural resources was the passage of the *Natural Resources Act* of 1941, which granted a national Natural Resources Board sweeping authority to manage environmental resources. Regulations governing cutting of trees, grazing and soil conservation fell within the ambit of the board, to the point of obliging local villagers to perform forced labour for designated conservation actions. That Act continues to provide the legal framework through which a command-and-control management regime operates to this day in communal areas (Scoones and Matose 1995).

Through these restrictive measures, not to mention direct physical coercion exercised over many decades, the African population was driven from the most productive soils and pushed to arid lands highly suscept-ible to fluctuations in rainfall and climatic conditions. In fact, by 1950 approximately 30 per cent of the population was landless (Moyo 1991). Moreover, the land alienation process disrupted indigenous systems of land and resource management.

For the white settler economy, largely oriented to export markets, growth of the large-scale agricultural farms quickly spawned expansion of agroprocessing plants for cotton, livestock and sugar-based products, from which subsequent industrial diversification could take place. The mining sector also expanded steadily. Still constrained by limitations imposed on mining activities by the BSAC, the settler government literally purchased the colony's mining rights in 1930 to open mining opportunities to the growing immigrant population. In periods of economic contraction such as during the 1930s, Europeans moved into the small-scale mining arena working placer gold deposits. By the late 1940s, large mining concerns extracting gold, chrome and iron ore, among others, gained dominance in the mining sector, often attracting foreign investment. Steel and iron plants were built during the 1930s and 1940s, allowing the country to become a producer of intermediate capital goods, which also served as the basis for further industrial diversification.

In this increasingly diversified economy, manufactures surpassed the contribution of primary sectors to the economy by the 1940s. By 1965, the manufacturing sector's contribution had risen to 40 per cent of total exports, which included important sub-sectors in metal products and chemicals in addition to the consumer goods. The economic under-pinnings in the agricultural sector, pitting large-scale settler farming against the small-scale and communal production of Africans, remained untouched. The disparities in the land regime also extend to the forestry and the wildlife sectors, equally dominated by commercial settler interests.

Unilateral Declaration of Independence (UDI)

As decolonization moved southwards on the African continent during the 1950s and 1960s, virtually surrounding Southern Rhodesia, a strong case was made among settlers for loosening the economic stranglehold of the white community, opening economic opportunities to the black majority, and even encouraging emergence of an African economic elite in the country. It was, however, the intransigence of the settler community in its unwillingness to expand political participation to the Africans that galvanized the whites in their decision to unilaterally declare independence from Britain. With its 'go it alone' policy slogan during the 1962 elections, the Rhodesian Front awaited only the most advantageous time and terms on which to issue the UDI in 1965.

In the wake of international condemnation and subsequent imposi-tion of economic sanctions on the breakaway colony, the settler community had little option but to pursue an import substitution industrialization policy. Yet the fact that industrial diversification had progressed so far by 1965 allowed Rhodesia to sustain its inwardly-focused economy for the better part of the next 15 years (Skälnes 1995). The status of the African population during the UDI phase changed little from the settler period. Infrastructure investments met the needs of the European producers, not the rural African communities. Prices for agricultural goods were biased against African producers, credit remained closed to native entrepreneurs and farmers, and social services provided to African communities lagged far behind the scope and calibre of those provided to the European population. The European domination of the economic, political and social systems remained absolute.

By the end of the 15-year period, the internal economic and political strains of maintaining the racially segregated regime rendered the international pariah an untenable enterprise. At the period's end, opportunities for further diversifying the economy had been exhausted, the need for foreign capital and technology increased, and the difficulty in accessing foreign markets constantly constrained economic opportunities. As conditions for the predominantly rural African population worsened, their willingness to embrace and actively support the growing guerrilla movement increased proportionately in both rural and urban communities. And for the African population, the promise of regaining control of the land was the single most important motivation that drove the rural population to support ZANU, ZAPU (Zimbabwe African People's Union) and other groups in their armed struggle.

Independence

In 1980, as today, the land question and access to natural resources was central to determining the development path of the country. At the time of independence, the policy makers of ZANU-PF were pulled between two fundamental, often conflicting, development options. The first development option would be shaped by responding to the requirements of the white corporate sector, including farmers, industrialists and financiers. The second path would require addressing the needs of the largely land-poor or landless Africans. Despite the initial Marxist-Leninist rhetoric accompanying the independence struggle, ZANU-PF pursued a markedly conservative economic policy during its first decade by ensuring the continued control of the European entrepreneurs and financiers over the economy. After the first wave of white flight in the early 1980s, approximately 110,000 settlers remained in Zimbabwe, down by almost 50 per cent from the pre-independence level, and reduced to only 1 per cent of the country's population. At that time, 6100 European commercial farmers controlled 39 per cent of the country's total land area and about two-thirds of the most productive lands on which they produced 80 per cent of the country's marketed agricultural output. European control over the manufacturing and financial sectors was even more absolute (World Bank 1995a). It was this economic structure that the nationalist government decided to protect during the first decade following independence.

While attending first to the economic needs of the white-dominated economy, ZANU-PF embarked on a programme to extend social services and some economic opportunities to the African population in communal areas. Communal areas included 700,000 smallholder households 'crowded into tribal trust land areas, most of which lay in semi-arid parts of the country or in locations with poor soils' (World Bank 1995a). Providing education and health services constituted the backbone of that greatly expanded service provision. Another central feature of the government's effort to support the rural African population was the extension of government marketing services to smallholder farmers through construction of maize and produce collection points in communal areas. Similarly, fixed or floor prices for most crops sought to guarantee minimal prices for poor farmers. While requiring consistently high subsidies, particularly in times of drought, the collection system and marketing boards proved important in the 1980s in providing economic opportunities to rural populations previously outside the formal economy. The costs of those subsidies, however, weighed heavily on government budgets as recovery from the global recession lagged and budget deficits mounted, ultimately obliging the government to undertake structural reforms by the early 1990s.

The government initiated modest land redistribution efforts in the first five years following independence. In the 1980s the government of Zimbabwe had purchased or obtained through forfeiture over 3 million hectares of land on which 47,678 families were resettled by the end of the decade. During the 1980s, the government tried to open lands to a very small but growing black elite. For example, during the first decade following independence, over 400 blacks were given loans through the Agricultural Finance Corporation to acquire large-scale commercial farms ranging from 500 to 5000 hectares. Moreover, communal co-operatives gained access to 176,000 hectares while state-owned farms controlled about 500,000 hectares of land (Moyo 1995).

Other changes took place in government land policy during the 1980s that contrasted sharply with the promises extended to ex-comba-

tants of the independence struggle. Rather than expanding land redistribution as a central part of the state's growing control over economic
activities, the government actually halved its land acquisition budget by
1988, signalling to large-scale commercial farmers, that is the settler
community, that their commercial ventures remained secure. During the
late 1980s the government constrained the availability of credit, reduced
fertilizer and other inputs, and limited the availability of seeds to smallholders, further limiting their economic opportunities (World Bank
1995).

Government control over other lands, as with other parts of the
economy, expanded during the 1980s. Perhaps the most important step
in increasing state control over the smallholder sector was the *Communal
Lands Act* of 1982 by which government extended its political and
economic control over communal areas. This and other legislative means
reduced the power of traditional chiefs, as the control of district rural
councils and other administrators appointed by the government
increased commensurately. As government involvement in communal
areas increased, the government offered few if any comprehensive proposals to address the stark inequities between white commercial farmers,
still holding lands acquired almost a century earlier, and communal areas
that felt the increasing pressures of environmental degradation and
demographic growth. Moreover, public distrust of the ZANU-PF government increased in the late 1980s, when it became apparent that the land
redistribution programmes were benefiting party functionaries, government ministers and high-ranking civil servants. Growing cronyism
and corruption within the ranks of government stirred the anger of
urban dwellers, both black and white, while neglect of the communal
areas further exacerbated environmental degradation and poverty in rural
areas.

Control and management of forests reflected the basic pattern
associated with land tenure in the years following independence. The
forest management regime was inherited directly from the colonial and
UDI periods in which two distinct tenurial and management systems
were implemented. Large-scale commercial farms were entrusted to
manage their forested areas on a self-policing basis on the assumption
that these farms would maximize forest cover for both profit and

resource protection. Legislation also provided mechanisms by which the large-scale farms could produce products for commercial markets.

Forests in the communal areas, in contrast, were subject to increased state regulation and control, limiting forest use to subsistence purposes and forbidding communities from marketing timber. Moreover, rural district councils, responsible for managing the forest estate in communal areas, were not given financial resources to promote reforestation programmes and sustainable use. The outcome of this dualistic policy has been a pattern of increasing forest degradation in and adjacent to communal areas, with villagers often obliged to cut wood and harvest crops within state forest estates (Nhira et al 1998; Mandondo 2000).

ECONOMIC REFORMS

The Need to Reform

Unlike many structural reforms in Africa, Zimbabwe's programme did not open with an IMF stabilization programme. In fact, the government did not face imminent financial or economic collapse, nor were structural imbalances of such magnitude that urgency was required in promoting economic reforms. However, there was a clear need to move away from the import substitution industrialization model of the UDI, to open the economy to foreign capital and foreign markets, and to reform exchange rate policy, while also reducing fiscal imbalances associated with parastatals and public sector employment. These structural bottlenecks were slowly sapping the economy of its vitality. For example, by the end of the 1980s total investment had fallen to less than 20 per cent of GDP and was insufficient to raise productivity. Moreover, growth in the labour force greatly outpaced the expansion of employment opportunities, thus intensifying pressure in rural areas and pushing tens of thousands of unemployed people into the informal sector. Hence the challenge was to embark on a steady liberalization programme that would allow the industrial, agricultural and mining sectors to expand by tapping into new international markets (World Bank 1995a; Gibbon 1995).

Faced with the prospects of continued stagnation, the private sector, dominated by white economic interests, gave the impetus for structural reforms in Zimbabwe. In particular, the Confederation of Zimbabwe Industries promoted a gradualist approach to economic reforms, trying to win white farmers, the financial sector and, ultimately, the government to the imperative of liberalizing the economy (Skälnes 1995). Proponents of reform slowly overcame initial resistance from various economic sectors as the economy continued to suffer from an overvalued currency, import controls and a lack of investment capital. With the private sector aligned behind the liberalization strategy, resistance from within government also diminished as growing budget deficits, deepening balance of payments problems and declining donor support fuelled economic crisis and growing political discontent in urban populations. These parties agreed, in consonance with the recommendations of World Bank missions, that the locally-designed and -initiated adjustment programme should focus initially on fiscal, trade and domestic regulatory policies, coupled with social mitigation programmes to address the potential negative social impacts of the reform process (World Bank 1991, 1995b; Gibbon 1995).

The government began implementation of the Economic Structural Adjustment Programme (ESAP), the first phase of the adjustment process, in 1990 and during the subsequent six years sought to achieve the following objectives.

- Reduce budget deficits and reform public enterprise. To this end, the government sought to reduce the crowding out of private investment by public sector debt, reduce non-interest expenditures, cut back subsidies to state-owned businesses and to reduce the size of the civil service and the government's role in wage setting.
- Liberalize the trade regime. To improve Zimbabwe's competitiveness and access to foreign exchange, the government restructured import tariffs and licensing arrangements.
- Increase domestic competitiveness. To this end the reform dismantled the restrictive foreign exchange allocation system, decontrolled current account transactions, capital transactions and domestic prices, and phased out consumer subsidies.

- Strengthen social safety nets to help protect the poor. The social mitigation activities tried to address the impacts of civil service cutbacks, higher inflation, removal of subsidies and phasing-in of user fees.

The Zimbabwe Programme for Economic and Social Transformation (ZIMPREST), the second phase of the reform process, was launched in 1996. While continuing efforts to maintain macroeconomic stability, ZIMPREST reinforced plans to open the economy to world markets. It also called for increased investment to expand entrepreneurial opportunities for black-owned businesses and to create employment opportunities for the black population. Policy makers also included specific initiatives for mining, agriculture and manufacturing, leaving aside specific policy plans for tourism.

We should first point out the positive economic outcomes resulting from the reform programmes. Foremost, reforms helped expand Zimbabwe's exports to include a wider range of manufactured goods and agricultural products. Export of manufactured goods rose 14 per cent per year between 1991 and 1996 and agricultural exports grew by 43 per cent per year between 1991 and 1996, a total of 305 per cent. GDP growth accelerated to more than 5 per cent per year between 1992 and 1995 and investments rose to about 22 per cent of GDP. Moreover, Zimbabwe's economic outlook improved substantially after the implementation of the second set of reforms in 1996, particularly in the manufacturing sector, as foreign and domestic investors brought money back into the economy. The country's labour costs were now globally competitive, and two excellent rainy seasons boosted agricultural production, thereby generating benefits that rippled throughout the entire economy. Government expenditures declined as 23,000 civil service jobs were eliminated and a further 12,000 posts were cut from the military.

While the aim of economic reforms was to increase overall economic efficiency and accelerate economic growth, a striking feature is that economic performance has deteriorated on many counts since the launch of the reforms. GDP per capita in 1997 was still well below pre-liberalization levels while budget deficits continued at approximately 8 per cent, the same level as a decade earlier. Inflation increased from 14 per cent in 1990 to more than 18 per cent in 1997. There has been a distributional shift away from low-income employed households to profit earners as a result of the soaring inflation and also stagnant output and employment (World Bank 1997; ZERO 2000). A steep rise in the price of the average household food basket, the reduction of food subsidies and a 35 per cent decline in wages reduced real income and deepened the breadth of poverty, particularly in the countryside. Spending on health and education fell drastically, threatening the impressive social welfare improvements made since independence.

The economy worsened dramatically in the last years of the 1990s as political and economic setbacks brought the country to the brink of collapse. Inflation reached 60 per cent in 2000 and foreign reserves were depleted, rendering the importation of petroleum and other basic necessities increasingly difficult. Heavy borrowing continued to sustain government spending but, in turn, created extremely high interest rates, reduced the availability of private credit, halted investment initiatives and dampened domestic demand. Contributing to the economic collapse was Zimbabwe's involvement in the war in the Democratic Republic of Congo, and non-compliance with IMF lending terms and the subsequent suspension of disbursements, as well as the political turmoil associated with the elections of 2000 and thereafter.

Impact of Structural Reforms on Tourism

We focused the Zimbabwean sectoral study on tourism for several reasons, including its central importance to many rural communities and its direct link to the land question, the resolution of which will determine the welfare of millions of Africans. Moreover, the tourism sector experienced a significant expansion that helped carry the Zimbabwean economy through the uncertainties of the reform process. It thus seemed that if economic reforms were to generate benefits for the rural population it would be through the tourism sector. In particular, the well-known CAMPFIRE programme, acronym for Communal Areas Management Programme for Indigenous Resources, seemed to be a likely mechanism by which those benefits would reach communal areas. CAMPFIRE was organized on the premise that '"producer communities" or the basic units of social organization in wildlife-rich areas should be empowered to use and manage the resources' (Mandondo 2000).

The government and World Bank did not anticipate sustained expansion of the tourism sector as they agreed on the basic elements of the structural adjustment programme in the early 1990s, despite the fact that during the previous decade the tourism industry grew by 192 per cent while the rest of the economy grew 48 per cent. Their lack of attention to the sector was reflected in the failure to develop a sectoral development strategy and implementation plan for the duration of reform's first phase.

Despite that oversight, in a matter of several years the sector rose to be the fourth largest contributor to GDP. Tourism's contribution to GDP increased from 2.6 per cent in 1992 to 7 per cent in 1996, putting it just behind manufacturing, mining and agriculture. Between 1991 and 1997, revenue from tourism increased 400 per cent and the number of tourists entering Zimbabwe increased 300 per cent. Apart from South Africa, Zimbabwe was the only sub-Saharan country to receive over one million tourists in 1994. When its secondary benefits (such as associated and informal employment for artisans and farmers) are taken into account, its contribution to the economy almost doubled. Industry employment figures show an increase in jobs from 40,532 in 1990 to 83,400 in 1995, a 105 per cent increase, and tourism jobs represent about a third of all employment in the service sector. The total tax yield from tourism increased from 229.4 million Zimbabwe dollars in 1990 to 1.1 billion in 1995. Earnings from tourism were equivalent to about 10 per cent of all exported goods and services, making tourism the third largest foreign exchange earner after mining and agriculture (ZERO 2000).

Three Local Experiences

With these considerable sectoral improvements providing a national economic backdrop, the expectation that benefits would accrue to the rural villages deeply involved in trophy hunting and non-consuming tourism seemed reasonable. ZERO, an environmental non-governmental organization, conducted an inquiry into the impact of the expanding tourist economy on four wards in the southeastern part of the country (ZERO 2000). These sites were considered representative of conditions found in many communities that are located near national tourist parks where smallholder agricultural production predominates yet where large-scale tourist activities are common. In addition to gathering data about the tourism incomes in the villages, they sought to understand if and how adjustment, particularly the resulting expansion of tourism sector, created more economic opportunities for communities or, in contrast, intensified conflicts between communities and neighbouring national parks.

Foremost, data gathered in the four wards led researchers to conclude that growth in tourism was not felt on the local level in this part of the country. Although several wards bordered national parks, neither employ-ment nor spin-off economic benefits accrued to the villages. They also underscored the costs, such as loss of livestock and crops to wildlife, which are associated with supporting tourism at the village level.

Respondents in three wards confirmed that in years past CAMP-FIRE programmes provided an important source of cash income for the villagers. The study likewise confirmed the lack of power exercised by local communities over resources, land, distribution and use of tourism benefits, while rural district councils – essentially political extensions of the ruling party – increased their control over local resource manage-ment. Despite explicit policies to enhance local control, the *Rural District Councils Act* passed in 1988 'deracialized local government [but] it did not decentralize or democratize it – the Act, in fact, recentralized power at the district level, whilst making the exercise of such power unilateral, top-down, and undemocratic' (Mandondo 2000).

Moreover, the local studies confirmed a more general tension in communal areas across the country as the economic contraction and layoffs associated with the adjustment programme intensified downward pressure on the incomes of the rural poor. The adverse economic condi-tions resulted in 'increased migration back to communal areas, resettle-ment areas, and small-scale commercial farms where population pressures were already placing a heavy burden on the fragile ecosystems and scarce natural resources' (ZERO 2000). This outcome further intensified widespread negative impacts on communal areas already under enormous pressures from demographic growth and environmental degradation.

A parallel study conducted by WWF on the future of tourism and sport hunting in Zimbabwe highlighted a number of factors that limited the adoption of wildlife as viable land use for communal areas (Bond 1997). Those limitations arise from the expansion of agropastoral production systems, institutional arrangements and broader economic conditions. As stated, those constraints include:

- the breakdown of both the traditional and modern political mechanisms for the allocation of land;
- the low rate of return to individual households from wildlife utilization in the communal lands;
- the failure to genuinely empower rural wildlife producer communities; and
- the increasing demand for any form of land due to the declining real urban wages and (declining) probability of employment in the formal sector.

The study points out the rising importance of tourism for the large-scale commercial farms (LSCF) sector and the increased opportunities for non-consuming wildlife tourism as a complementary source of income for commercial farmers. The study also notes the declared policy that state protected areas will constitute the core of sport hunting in the country.

A third study introduces a new factor into the equation, the role of national and international tourist operators and their interaction with communal areas (Murphree 2001). The study focuses on the financial viability of a CAMPFIRE programme in Mahenye, a community located in the southeastern part of the country along the border with Mozambique. In its early years, the experience of Mahenye could be considered typical, in that promises made during the war of liberation to devolve land to the community were not respected, while constant government interference throttled community efforts to develop tourist opportunities. Those problems gave rise to numerous struggles with government offices and park officials over poaching, damage caused by wildlife and concession revenues.

That situation changed under the structural reform programme when Zimbabwe Sun expressed interest in developing tourist lodges on communal lands and with the Save Valley Conservancy. It should be noted that the Save Valley Conservancy, the largest conservancy in the world covering 3200 square kilometres, is a holding company consisting of 17 LSCFs joined together for 'corporate management of natural resources' (Moyo 2000). Complex negotiations gave rise to formal agreement in 1996 by which the community would leave areas of communal land free from human habitation and disturbances. In return for leaving the land undisturbed for wildlife tourism, Zimbabwe Sun would pay the rural district council an established percentage of gross revenues over a ten-year period.

The returns to the communal area have been considerable and, in addition to the revenues distributed to the council, have included improved road transport, electrical power, telephone connections, water reticulation and employment for a limited number of local people. The distribution of revenues has risen considerably over the years the agreement has been in effect. The study also underscores the contentious legal and structural problems between the community and government offices that beset the Mahenye experience as well as the CAMPFIRE experience more generally (Murphree 2001).

Under Adjustment's Shadow

Explaining these different outcomes as regards distribution of benefits from tourism growth under the structural reforms, ie that many communal areas seem to have been bypassed while only a limited number of areas have enjoyed spin-off benefits, obliges us to look at the broader changes in land use in association with the structural adjustment process. A coherent analytical framework for understanding those outcomes, and for understanding the skewed distribution of benefits from the adjustment process more generally, is provided by Sam Moyo (2000). His analysis also provides a framework for understanding the political dynamics associated with the land question that have resulted in the country's political paralysis and economic collapse.

The starting point of Moyo's analysis is his assertion that structural reforms have had significant impact on land uses and values. The change in land uses and values has resulted primarily from liberalization of domestic agricultural markets, provision of numerous export incentives, and reduction of financial and import/export controls so that foreign capital could enter and leave the country more easily. Liberalization of domestic commodities markets, opening the country to international markets, and new assurances to foreign investors have provided a set of incentives that have led landowners to diversify production into higher value products and activities. Specific agricultural sector reforms have deepened these effects of macroeconomic changes by loosening governmental control over commodity prices, marketing arrangements and credit mechanisms (World Bank 1995a).

Coupled with the *Land Act* of 1992, which was designed prior to the implementation of the reform package, restructuring of the agricultural sector led to a significant change in land use, particularly in large-scale commercial farms and state-owned farms. Moyo highlights how landowners responded to the new incentives associated with the adjustment process by shifting to horticulture production, wildlife and ostrich raising and away from lower value crops such as tobacco and cotton. Case studies identify trends in the three forms of land ownership – LSCF, state estates and communal areas – as regards their adoption of new land uses and production options. Moreover, the studies present data on returns to producers, destinations of products, forms of tourism and returns to communal areas from these new forms of land use.

From the empirical evidence, Moyo draws several important conclusions as regards the impact of structural reforms on land use and associated economic benefits. 'More large than small farmers engage in these new land uses on much larger areas than small farmers. Even among blacks, the elite have taken up the new land uses more rapidly.' These land use changes have been adopted by approximately 50 per cent of LSCF, but no more than 10 per cent of communal areas are engaged in new land uses. The most significant shift in communal areas has been to horticulture production that is credited with improving household incomes. These shifting land uses, particularly for ostrich production and wildlife, have taken hold in state-run estates as well.

Moyo makes clear that these changes are directly associated with Zimbabwe's deeper integration into the global market system:

> Since ESAP deepened the monetarist system of macro-economic management and market-based social relations of production, Zimbabwe has experienced change in land property relations, commodity trade systems involving a wide range of land products, rural labour management, and the appropriation and application of new agrarian technologies. The basic motives for and organization of land-related primary economic production systems have changed mainly in response to new global markets and geo-political relations.

These new land uses and higher returns have significantly altered the dynamics of the land market and altered the political struggles unfolding around the land question. Moyo identifies several key trends:

- Subdivision of large commercial farms. With higher returns, farmers can maintain income levels by intensifying production on a smaller amount of land, thereby allowing for the sale of underutilized land to new entrepreneurs. Subdivision is also occurring in peri-urban areas.
- Entry of black entrepreneurs on state-owned land. The government has granted leaseholds to black farmers entering large-scale commercial farming and provided subsidies and credit to support their start-up operations.
- Entry of transnational corporations. Large-scale corporate arrangements combining national and transnational corporations have entered the land market, promoting new land uses including tourism, niche produce and wildlife farming.
- Illegal allocation of communal lands. As demand for land has increased and prices have hardened, illegal mechanisms of conveying land in communal areas to persons outside the areas have increased.
- Increased investment on state-owned lands. The Forest Commis-

sion, Parks Authority, and estate farms have increased investments in
new land use activities, thereby hardening the government's reluct-
ance to redistribute land.

- Utilization of marginal lands. The introduction of new land uses,
  particularly wildlife and tourism, has increased the value of previously unused lands. These lands have been offered on the market for
  purchase by international corporations and national entrepreneurs.
- Self-provisioning. A euphemism for squatter occupations, as land-
  poor Africans have taken into their own hands the seizure of lands
  from the state, LSCFs and communal areas.

Political Manipulation of the Land Question

The issue of self-provisioning, or land seizures, is central to understanding the distributional effects of the adjustment process. It is also the
key to understanding the political crisis and economic collapse consum-
ing the country at the beginning of the new millennium. As pointed out
earlier, the designers of the adjustment process in the government and
World Bank had no intention of restructuring the land tenure and
natural resource ownership regimes. To the contrary, their shared interest
was increasing the productivity of the industrial and agricultural sectors,
largely of the white-dominated economy, and for the government,
increasing the economic influence of an emerging African economic elite
supported by the ruling party.

Because of the studious disregard of the land question under the
reform process, crisis conditions and pent-up demand for land in communal areas invariably led to growing social unrest in rural areas from the
early 1990s onward. Moreover, the demands of the rural poor, representing 80 per cent of country's poor, converged at that time with the interests of a growing black economic nationalist lobby, largely urban based,
which wanted to increase the access of its elite members to the country's
most productive lands.

Those growing public pressures obliged the government to convene
a national commission in the early 1990s to articulate new government
policy regarding the land question, ultimately giving rise to a second

phase of the country's land reform process. As a result, the government enacted 'constitutional amendments removing restrictions on land acquisition and compensation, a new land policy statement in 1990, and the *Land Acquisition Act* of 1992' (Moyo 1995). Through those new measures the government broke with its earlier land redistribution policies, ie the market-based willing-seller/willing-buyer approach, established when the country became independent a decade earlier. Specifically, the new set of policies established the means by which the government could acquire land for redistribution and compensate owners. In a first effort to match its words with action, the government proceeded to redistribute 70 large commercial farms to the land poor in 1993 (Akwabi-Ameyaw 1997).

This effort to redistribute commercial farms to Africans did not dampen the growing desperation of the rural poor. Despite public pronouncements and promises, the new government land policy did little if anything to address the broader needs of the landless and land-poor in communal areas, areas that had absorbed tens of thousands of urban workers laid off during the adjustment process. Rather than directly addressing the needs of the growing number of rural poor, the government gave priority to fostering development of the black elite as a minority but emerging economic force in the LSCF sector (Moyo 1995). This approach required not only redistribution of land actually held by the state and appropriation of some additional white farmlands, but provision of subsidies, inputs and marketing opportunities over a number of years to ensure the economic success of that emergent black elite. As Moyo points out, however, the investment required to foster expansion of the black elite created direct competition for the government resources demanded by the communal areas. Moreover, during this period the government did not support efforts of the rural poor to seize control of underutilized commercial or state-owned lands, often evicting the squatters on these lands through physical and legal means.

Although this ZANU-PF policy may have increased support among the emerging black elite, tensions exacerbated significantly with the rural poor whose land demands had not been addressed. In response to the growing resentment among the rural poor, ZANU-PF's traditional political base, President Robert Mugabe travelled across the country during 1997–98 promising rural populations that the government would seize half of the country's white-owned farms, without compensation, to resettle tens of thousands of landless peasants. Not surprisingly then, during mid-1998, land invasions of white-owned farms involving several thousand peasants in the northeastern part of the country catapulted the land issue to national prominence. Similar squatter actions followed shortly thereafter near Bulawayo in Mashonaland, and Manicaland, raising the prospects of uncontrolled land seizures, broader social upheaval, and loss of political control by the central government. To placate the restive landless squatters, and to allay the rising discontent among international donors, the government outlined a five-year plan that would resettle 100,000 families (800,000 people) on five million hectares of land purchased from white farmers (Economist Intelligence Unit 1998–2000).

ZANU-PF's rhetoric and political manipulation of the land question during the 2000 parliamentary elections only raised its prominence on the national political agenda. To mobilize its rural political base for electoral purposes, President Mugabe and his party encouraged and engineered land invasions that were frequently accompanied by violence, beatings and murder of white farmers, black farmhands and political opponents. In the context of political competition associated with elections, the ruling party promised to redistribute over five million hectares of prime farmland, thereby reducing the LSCF sector by 50 per cent to six million hectares. Legal steps to seize 841 properties covering 2.1 million hectares were approved by the legislative branch in mid-2000, opening the path to immediate redistribution (Economist Intelligence Unit 1998–2000).

Towards Resolution or Protracted Conflict?

ZANU-PF's increasingly radical rhetoric during the latter half of the 1990s, coupled with nominal land redistribution policies, contained the mounting anger of the rural poor. More recently, President Mugabe's political pronouncements, the violent actions of ZANU-PF militants in seizing white farms, the subsequent threats to white industrialists and aggressive acts toward the diplomatic corps have moved to the centre of the political crisis and media attention.

It is, however, the deepening of inequality in the rural sector and the economic duress in communal areas that created social conditions in which political crisis became unavoidable. At the centre of that growing inequality is the increased economic benefit derived from new land uses for the wealthy, particularly white and emergent black farmers, for international corporations and for the political elite affiliated with the ruling party. On the other hand, the growing economic, environmental and social crisis that prevails in the communal areas drives and will continue to drive efforts by the poor to obtain the productive resources on which their survival depends.

The three case studies on the impact of tourism on land use and land markets under adjustment, microcosms of the broader dynamics in rural areas, illustrate the skewed distribution of benefits resulting from the economic reform programme. LSCFs and the state estate sector have responded most directly to the new incentives created under the economic liberalization programme. They have actively responded by investing in new tourism programmes, generating considerable economic benefit for both the investing companies and the aggregate economy. Communal areas have not been able to respond directly; instead, they have derived benefits primarily when scant opportunities trickle down from the LSCF and state sectors.

In responding to the new economic opportunities, the more dynamic economic agents have substantially altered land uses and land markets across the country and increased their economic presence in rural areas. In contrast, the communal areas, limited by institutional conditions imposed by the government and their lack of capital, have been significantly constrained in responding to new opportunities. For them the economic reform programme has weakened their competitive abilities in the emerging market environment and obliged them to rely ever more intensely on natural resources for their survival.

At some point in the not-too-distant future, the current political regime will be replaced by a new government, hopefully one more broadly based and representative. Unknown, of course, are the total costs of the political transition process in economic, social and political terms. Those costs notwithstanding, the economic structures put in place by the adjustment process will, in one form or another, provide the economic incentives and institutional context in which economic agents will try to rekindle the Zimbabwean economy.

What we derive from this brief discussion about structural change, tourism and changing land uses is that the economic reform programme, through its impact on the land market, has had a direct and significant impact on the welfare of the poor. Above all, the reforms directly influence the ability of the landless and land-poor to control environmental resources on which their livelihoods directly depend. Unless a very explicit social policy is effected to condition the implementation of economic programmes, those impacts will continue to vest greater control and wealth in the powerful, privileged sectors of the economy while reducing the options and competitive capacity of the rural smallholder sector.

The point to be highlighted in closing is that the pursuit of macroeconomic equilibria and 'getting the prices right' is not only an insufficient approach for addressing rural poverty and environmental sustainability; it can also quickly move a society in the opposite direction unless proper institutional and political conditions prevail. Foremost among those required conditions are:

- economic incentives and subsidies explicitly directed to strengthening the competitive capacity of the rural poor;
- institutional conditions in place by which the rural poor can stabilize and strengthen control over environmental assets; and
- political systems guaranteeing the inclusion and proper representation of the rural poor.

In addition to the challenges of moving beyond the political impasse engulfing Zimbabwean society is the complex task of addressing the deepening inequalities and conflicts in rural areas. In that regard, we believe the greatest risk will be that, rather than responding to the structural problems in rural areas caused by adjustment, the political excesses of the current regime will become the scapegoat for Zimbabwe's crisis. Indeed, there is little difficulty in pointing out how the political manipulations of the past decade have accentuated inequities in Zimbabwean society. Beyond these obvious manipulations, however, the country must come to grips with the impact of structural reforms on the rural poor, on the skewed distribution of opportunity, the growing influence of commercial interests in rural areas, and the declining control of the rural poor over environmental resources. Addressing those issues will be major challenges for Zimbabwe's diverse civil society and community-based organizations during and after the transition to a new political regime.

Chapter 5

Natural Resource Wealth in the Construction of Neoliberal Economies in Southern Africa

*With Ola Larsson**

In this final essay we draw on the three country experiences to offer more general observations about economic reforms, governance and natural resource wealth in southern Africa. Consistent with the political economy perspective presented in the first pages of these essays, we try to understand the interaction of social groups, economic agents and the state in their pursuit of power and wealth associated with natural resources as these countries have undergone changes in their economic structures.

We have organized these conclusions around two basic questions:

1   What groups or economic agents have gained or lost control over natural resources in the context of the economic reforms?

* Ola Larsson served as coordinator of WWF's Macroeconomic Reforms and Sustainable Development in Southern Africa project from 1997–2000. He holds an MS in economics from the University of Stockholm and is currently a project manager for Kairos Future in Stockholm.

2   Through what processes, policies and relations have these actors acquired or lost control over those resources?

In addition, we have tried to respond to a third question that we answer from the perspective of an international environmental non-governmental organization:

3   Will those changes move the countries toward adopting more sustainable development paths by promoting environmental conservation, enhancing social equity and increasing public accountability and transparency of government activities and policies?

In closing, we offer some general observations about the reform process, notably regarding the consequences of implementing economic and institutional reforms without a national consensus to establish priorities and ensure public support. We also offer several recommendations regarding ways of addressing some of the negative outcomes experienced in the three countries.

Before embarking on this summary, we would like to rejoin the analytical framework sketched out in the first essay for interpreting the role of natural resource wealth in these economies of sub-Saharan Africa.

To begin, we need to return to the observation that structural reforms built on the basic elements of the Washington consensus and implemented during the past 20 years in developing and transition countries constitute the foundations of a global economic policy on which integration of the world economy is proceeding today. When the economic reforms were being designed in the early 1990s for these three African countries, the Washington consensus had firmly established its hold on policy making, and relatively little deviance from the prescripts of that consensus was tolerated. The three essential features of that prescription were:

1   To diminish the role of the state as an economic agent and establish private economic agents as the driving force in national economies.
2   To dismantle barriers to the international flow of goods and capital so that export-led growth drives national and global economic expansion.

3   To reform national institutions, including legal codes, regulatory systems and tenure regimes, among others, to support the economic reforms.

Despite declarations from the Bretton Woods institutions that the oft-maligned Washington consensus is dead, the fact remains that its essential policy features remain as much in effect today as when these three African countries embarked on their respective reform processes over a decade ago.

The statist economies maintained by authoritarian political regimes in southern Africa were incompatible with this reform blueprint on one fundamental point. Those regimes prevented private capital from gaining access to the countries' considerable natural resource wealth. State control blocked the entry of international corporations into those economies that were based on extensive and diverse resource wealth – minerals, fertile soils, fisheries, wildlife and forests – and allowed that wealth to be exploited by an increasingly corrupt national political elite.

Flowing from that incompatibility was a second major problem. Growing social inequities on global, regional and national levels and the prevalence of poverty posed direct challenges to the legitimacy of multilateral development agencies responsible for overseeing implementation of that global economic blueprint. Public resources were being used to finance structural reform programmes and development projects that, particularly as regards low-income countries, frequently brought no apparent amelioration in the plight of the poor despite improvement in traditional economic indicators. To counterbalance that record, the economic reform programmes had to demonstrate tangible results in alleviating poverty, particularly in contrast to the accumulation of wealth in urban areas and Northern societies more generally. Achieving that outcome was not possible under the autocratic regimes that dominated the resource-based countries of southern Africa.

The twin imperatives of opening these resource-rich economies to international capital and reversing the growing social inequities shaped the policy interventions of the Bretton Woods institutions. The experiences examined in these essays highlight the fact that the Bretton Woods institutions designed and oversaw economic reform programmes assuming the presence of economic and institutional conditions that simply did not exist in the three countries. Moreover, despite the fact that the countries had large rural populations living in abject poverty and their economies were built on resource wealth managed under autocratic political systems, the development institutions still expected the outcomes to parallel those of countries with more diversified economies and more democratic systems of governance. That the outcomes have proven less than satisfactory, even in terms of traditional economic indicators, should not be surprising.

QUESTION 1: WHAT GROUPS OR ECONOMIC AGENTS HAVE GAINED OR LOST CONTROL OVER NATURAL RESOURCES IN THE CONTEXT OF ECONOMIC REFORMS?

The changes in resource control and access were varied and complex, yet moved generally toward placing control of natural resources in private hands.

From the State to Private Economic Agents

The principal transfer of control over environmental resources was from the state to private corporations and individuals. That transfer, however, had numerous dimensions. First, recipients of those transfers were international corporations, often foreign-based, that entered the countries with considerable investment capital and ample access to international markets. Those corporations included mining companies and tourist concessions in Tanzania; agribusiness, forest and mining companies, and tourist concessions in Zambia; and tourist and agribusiness in Zimbabwe. These multinational companies acquired rights to extract minerals and timber and to develop lodges and accommodations in high-value tourist destinations, and acquired land titles or concessions for large-scale commercial agriculture and logging.

Second, transfers of state-owned resources included granting mining and tourist concessions to national entrepreneurs on a scale smaller than for the multinational corporations. Transfers were carried out through grants of prospecting and mining concessions and concessions for modest tourist accommodations and access to national parks and protected areas. Transfers also included grants of land concessions to medium-sized commercial farms, often on lands previously managed and controlled by rural communities, as was the case in Zambia. Such was also the experience with forested areas in Zambia that once were managed by traditional authorities. In Zimbabwe, the state provided long-term leases, subsidies and credit to a small group of black entrepreneurs seeking to establish large-scale commercial farms.

Third, transfers of state-controlled environmental resources included devolving ownership, or trusteeship, to villages, small farmers and the landless. Tanzania's land reform programme opened opportunities for millions of rural inhabitants to manage, securitize and invest in land and natural resources on that land. Mining reforms in Tanzania also allowed small-scale miners to stake claims in many rural areas deemed to be mineral rich. Effective control over many of those claims, however, was frequently unclear and subject to negotiation and/or legal action.

Transfer of Traditionally-Managed Resources to Private Control

With the implementation of legal and land tenure reforms, private companies and individuals were able to gain control over communally-controlled lands in Zambia. Frequently, neither the institutional mechanisms nor policy makers associated with those transactions were publicly accessible, nor were community authorities able to seek or obtain redress for these changes. This transfer from traditional to private control happened in other ways too. For example, with liberalization of the economy, small-scale tour operators from South Africa began operations in the rural areas of Zambia. Rural Zambians had not engaged in tourism activities of this kind prior to the reforms and were not prepared for or able to respond to the new activity in their traditional areas. Similarly, liberalization of Zimbabwe's land markets increased competition for new land and resulted in appropriation of land in communal areas through less than transparent means by private agents.

Transfer Between Private Owners

Competition and conflicts in Zimbabwe's rural areas between large-scale commercial farms and the land poor intensified as a result of the reform process. Growing poverty and increased demographic pressure led local leaders and villagers to seize white-owned commercial farms. In efforts to maintain its dominant political position, the ruling party mobilized militants and party faithful to support, then spearhead, the land seizures. A significant number of commercial farms have been confiscated and distributed to new occupants including party faithful, communal leaders, community groups and black entrepreneurs. The final disposition of those lands is far from established and will be determined only over a period of years.

In summary, the principal direction of the transfer of control of natural resource wealth was from the state to private interests and individuals. The transfers took various forms as resources passed to large foreign corporations, national entrepreneurs and individuals with varying levels of investment capital. The transfers from commercial farms to individuals arose primarily from the deepening grip of poverty in communal areas and were justified on the principle of correcting historical injustices of the colonial period.

QUESTION 2: THROUGH WHAT PROCESSES, POLICIES AND RELATIONS HAVE THESE GROUPS ACQUIRED OR LOST CONTROL OVER NATURAL RESOURCES?

Establishing the Neoliberal Policy Context

The three structural reform programmes crafted in accordance with the prescripts of the Washington consensus established the macroeconomic policies under which these transfers of natural resources took place. Those policies explicitly sought and succeeded, to varying degrees, in diminishing the role of the state as the organizing force of national economic life.

Establishing the policy context was accomplished primarily through the conditionalities imposed by the Bretton Woods institutions when they made financial resources available to the three governments. In some circumstances, such as the mining sector in Zambia, privatization of natural resource sectors was included as an explicit target of macro-economic reforms. Fulfilment of that conditionality became the requisite for releasing financial resources to the government and restructuring the country's privately held foreign debt.

In addition to the macroeconomic reforms, specific resource-based sectoral reforms, including reforms in agriculture, mining, tourism and forestry, explicitly sought to remove the state from economic activity in favour of private investors and entrepreneurs. These sectoral reform programmes established specific targets to guide withdrawal of the state and established a policy context, including fiscal incentives, institutional reforms and the removal of legal and financial barriers, which would ensure flexible operation of private enterprise.

Providing Guarantees and Incentives

The policy interventions of the Bretton Woods institutions were ultimately intended to create macroeconomic stability such that private capital, largely foreign in origin, would accept the risks associated with investing in the three countries. The conditions of private investors and lenders for investing in the countries were met through a series of policy and institutional commitments from which the three governments were highly reluctant to withdraw. The agreements with the Bretton Woods institutions provided the guarantees that would encourage private capital to assume the risks of returning to each country. Among those guarantees were reassurances that profits could be repatriated, that private banking firms could manage investment capital, that technology could be imported without undue constraint and delay, and that national currency could be converted to hard currency without constraint, among others. In addition, the reform process established a series of incentives that sought to ensure high returns for foreign investors. Among those incentives are numerous tax exemptions, explicit subsidies, exoneration from tariffs and duties, access to prime land and other tangible benefits. In essence, these incentives were designed to ensure investors that rents from natural resource sectors would be ample and continue over a sustained period of time.

Institutional Reforms

While macroeconomic and sectoral policies have been the focus of national and international attention, the wide range of institutional reforms accompanying the economic policies have been equally significant in changing access to and control over natural resource wealth. Institutional changes have, in general, followed implementation of economic policy reforms and are the mechanisms through which new policies are often felt most directly at the local level.

National-level institutional reforms enacted in the natural resource sectors of the three countries have included land reform, decentralization programmes, creation of resource authorities and political reforms of various kinds. In addition to the formal institutional reforms, the mechanisms by which access to natural resources are transferred or ceded to economic agents have changed as summarized below.

Land Reform

Each of the countries has implemented land reform programmes designed, in principle, to increase the access and control of smallholders, the land poor and the landless. In general, the reforms are premised on expanding market-based relations into rural areas, thereby supplanting the traditional forms of trusteeship and usufruct or overriding state-managed systems imposed following independence. The reforms do not promote private ownership of land as practised in Western societies; instead, they still vest ultimate ownership in the countries' presidents. They do, however, provide legal rights such that landholders are assured of long-term control and can, in some situations, use their land as collateral for credit purposes.

The forced land reform programme in Zimbabwe marks a departure from the approach followed in Tanzania and Zambia in that the government has sponsored a nationwide redistribution campaign of white-owned commercial farms. The land seizures are designed to redistribute settler farms to landless or land-poor Africans as a means of correcting the historical inequities inherited from the colonial and UDI periods. In fact, the coerced redistribution process has acquired dimensions of a political effort to perpetuate ZANU-PF's domination with as yet undetermined results in terms of increasing African villagers' control over the country's more productive lands.

Resource Authorities

Creation of resource authorities, as is the case with forests and wildlife in Zambia, is intended to increase the aggregate economic returns to the country from the exploitation of natural resources. These authorities, despite their proclaimed independence, remain under the management of political appointees allied with the ruling party. Moreover, while promising to increase revenues for local communities, the resource authorities have become mechanisms by which the central government can capture resource rents while offloading administrative costs from the central budget.

Decentralization

Decentralization has been embraced, in principle, by these African countries as they have attempted to move beyond the centralized, one-party rule of the post-colonial period. Decentralization implies devolving to local leaders and communities the authority to make decisions that affect their daily lives. However, as the case of Zambia illustrates, decentralization can be used to allay international and domestic concerns while maintaining centralized political control. In that country, symbolic political decentralization has not been accompanied by redistribution of government revenues, revenues to which local communities contribute through an array of taxes. Nor have local leaders been given the authority to establish new mechanisms to generate revenues, for example from wildlife, with which they could sponsor development projects. Moreover, the proposed decentralization process has provided a mechanism for marginalizing established local authorities from decision making while placing the political faithful and appointees in new positions of local power.

The more recent decentralization experience in Tanzania remains inconclusive, although there are promising signs that a more meaningful redistribution of decision making will accompany the ambitious land reform programme being implemented throughout the country.

In Zimbabwe, efforts to formally decentralize political authority have been subverted by the increased repression by the central government of political opposition movements. Paradoxically, the initiative taken by landless and the land poor to regain control over the land has placed these previously marginal groups at the centre of national political dynamics associated with the land question. Institutionalization of decentralized authority will be postponed until the current political and economic crises are resolved.

Corruption and Collusion

Corruption and collusion have accompanied changes in control over natural resources. Establishment of adequate institutional mechanisms to regulate and ensure transparency of transfers has not accompanied the process of privatizing the natural resources sectors. As a consequence, rampant corruption and collusion have characterized the reforms in every country and have taken many forms. Foremost, and perhaps most pernicious and difficult to identify, is the collusion between members of the country's political elite, either in dominant political parties or holding key positions in government agencies, and economic agents seeking access to natural resources. The results of this collusion take the form of granting mining concessions, construction permits on tourist sites, land grants or concessions on communal land, timber permits and tourist operator agreements, among many others.

These collusive arrangements, in the case of Tanzania and Zambia, have reached such proportions as to warrant national commissions and the establishment of corruption prevention boards. The pervasiveness of corruption is such that public confidence in all three governments has plummeted and provoked public protest and unrest. Moreover, international development agencies have threatened, and acted, to curtail financial assistance in the face of widespread public and private corruption.

The corruption at the national level invariably translates into comparable problems at the provincial, district and local levels. Whether seeking to gain access to village lands, mining sites, forests or wildlife, political authorities at these various levels have established privileged relations with new economic agents as they seek to invest in natural resource wealth while bypassing established authorities.

Coercion

Coercion, by which we mean the exercise of power to accomplish stated ends shared unequally by concerned stakeholders, had a constant presence prior to and during the reform process. For example, prior to the implementation of reform processes, coercion was a central factor in maintaining one-party regimes. As statist economies failed to deliver social and economic benefits to the public in the post-colonial period, elites relied to an increasing degree on multiple forms of repression and social control.

In the context of these authoritarian regimes, coercion exercised by international agencies was required to alter the political monopoly of one-party states and to create conditions under which economic reforms became possible. Such coercion was expressed through lending conditionalities' refusal to reschedule private debt obligations, and the terms of specific aid and investment programmes. As the World Bank and IMF frequently discovered, even that exercise of economic power had limited effect in trying to change the priorities, political processes and policies of autocratic regimes.

Coercion has been used frequently by national governments to repress civil society as it has risen up to protest against the social, political and environmental costs of the reform programmes. Authoritarian governments have used direct physical force, political repression, jailing and 'disappearances' to muzzle groups and individuals opposing economic reforms, corruption, the lack of democratic participation and the more general denial of human rights.

Of the three countries, the coercive measures employed, as a matter of policy, by the ruling party in Zimbabwe are unmatched in the region. Mobilization of party faithful to invade and seize white-owned commercial farms has expanded to include nationwide intimidation and repression of political opponents and attacks on white-owned industries and businesses as well. Not exempt from the systemic political repression are targeted groups from civil society and international NGOs. Escalation of coercion and physical violence is firmly engrained in the political dynamics unfolding across the country.

In summary, the Bretton Woods institutions established the economic policy framework, provided the guarantees to private investors, and helped to shape the institutional reforms through which the economic policies would be applied in each country. The establishment of the policy context and implementation of institutional reforms was rendered possible by the exercise of coercion that required governmental compliance to avoid financial and economic penalties. Those reform measures and institutional changes produced, in some cases, a significant improvement in traditional economic indicators. Moreover, some social groups benefited considerably from their new access to natural resource wealth while others, usually the rural poor, experienced heightened insecurity, falling living standards and weakened institutional control. As the policy and institutional reforms took hold, it also became apparent that numerous weaknesses and deficiencies allowed rampant corruption and collusion between political elites and new economic agents to thrive.

QUESTION 3: WILL THOSE CHANGES PROMOTE SUSTAINABLE DEVELOPMENT PATHS BY PROMOTING ENVIRONMENTAL SUSTAINABILITY, ENHANCING SOCIAL EQUITY AND INCREASING GOVERNMENTS' PUBLIC ACCOUNTABILITY?

Environmental Sustainability

The essays did not focus on the direct environmental impacts of the economic reforms in the specific resource sectors. We would, however, like to respond to the question at a somewhat higher level of generalization by asking if the economic reforms, new incentives and associated institutional changes succeeded in establishing economic and institutional conditions under which sustainable resource and environmental management will be likely to develop.

Our response to that question touches on four points. First, diminution of the state as a direct economic agent opens the possibility of establishing the state as the principal guarantor of national environmental performance and, subsequently, as a provider of public environmental goods and services. In years past, largely because of its direct investment in economic activities, the state in the three countries demonstrated an abiding lack of interest in establishing rigorous environmental management regimes to regulate economic activities. No case could be clearer than the environmental performance of Zambia's mining parastatals, which disregarded environmental concerns for decades despite widespread water, air and soil contamination around mining centres. With the state's diminished role as an economic agent, an important obstacle to developing a supportive environmental regime has been removed in large measure.

Second, despite the potential mentioned above, governments of the three countries are willing to pay an environmental price to attract foreign investors. One aspect of making the countries attractive investment targets is ensuring that the environmental standards with which investors must comply are minimal. For instance, although the Tanzanian mining code requires environmental impact assessments for all new mining operations, those statutory requirements have not been applied in granting concessions to medium- or large-scale mining companies. Similar conditions hold for the tourism sectors in Zimbabwe and Zambia, whereby governments have sought to increase domestic and international operations to support their struggling economies. Experience in the agricultural sector in Zambia follows the same pattern. More responsible multinational corporations, fearing the international consequences, have held themselves accountable to higher environmental standards than those established by host governments.

Third, collusion between government and the private sector discourages the development and application of rigorous environmental regulation. Party officials and government employees stand to derive direct benefits from natural resource wealth through kickbacks, side agreements and illicit joint ventures with private investors. These illegal activities create disincentives for the government to establish an effective environmental regulatory regime.

Fourth, the only sustained incentive to implement more rigorous environmental standards and establish more effective environmental agencies has come from external sources. There is no doubt that external resources have been extremely important in improving the environmental performance in all three countries, despite the fact that many direct outputs of those investments are for demonstration purposes and are often designed by the development agencies themselves.

Enhancing Social Equity

To date, the policy and sectoral reforms have brought occasional improvements in the welfare of rural populations. Land reform, decentralization, natural resource authorities and political changes promise to empower local producers, local communities and village authorities. However, those reforms, while benefiting some, have led to widespread uncertainty, insecurity and direct loss of control for a greater number of communities. In Tanzania, land reform holds the promise of improving opportunities for the rural poor, whereas in Zambia the potential gains of some entrepreneurs are eclipsed by the loss of control experienced by villagers and traditional authorities. In Zimbabwe, the economic reforms have not created conditions whereby the rural poor would gain greater control of environmental resources and increase their productive capacity. On the contrary, the reforms resulted in increased pressure on land through reinvigorated land markets in rural areas.

The economic reforms were justified over ten years ago by the promise that they would significantly improve the welfare of the rural poor by changing internal terms of trade, removing anti-rural biases and creating employment opportunities. Despite repeated declarations from the Bretton Woods institutions over the past decade that the economies are improving and per capita income is rising, the majority of Africans in each of the countries are still living in near-abject poverty. Reforms in natural resource sectors promised similar improvements in the lives of the rural poor and, with the exception of the mining sector in Tanzania, have delivered only meagre results.

Political Accountability and Transparency

The experience of the three countries is one of extreme contrasts and contradictions, with each country demonstrating stirrings of increased transparency coupled with a renewed embrace of authoritarianism and corruption. At one end of the spectrum, Tanzania has opened its formal political process to multi-party democracy, a freer press and more vibrant civil society. It has established mechanisms to address rampant corruption, has tried to promote the decentralization of decision making, and has renewed interest in increasing the 'voice' and viability of traditional chiefs. At the same time, however, the pervasiveness of corruption and rent seeking has severely undermined public confidence in the current system of governance, political parties and national leaders. The view that 'frontier economics', 'savage capitalism' and the emergence of a 'new mafia' have taken over Tanzanian economic life, often associated directly with natural resource sectors, is deeply felt in Tanzanian society.

Zambia, once held up as the beacon of democratic reform on the continent, has steadily slipped towards more autocratic rule since the implementation of economic reforms in the early 1990s. While NGOs proliferate in the capital and externally-funded health, welfare and environmental activities are distributed across the provinces, the formal mechanisms of governance have reverted to one-party domination and political manipulation. Accompanying the recentralization of political power, despite public decrees and laws to the contrary, is a growing collusion between the ruling party and private business that centres on the country's extensive natural resource wealth. Rural communities remain politically marginal except when national political dynamics require mobilization of the traditional leaders and villagers.

Zimbabwe falls into the other extreme of the spectrum as a society fractured by political strife, economic collapse and social instability related to the non-resolution of the land question, and associated natural resource issues. Political manipulation of the land question has led to increased assaults on the political opposition, compromising the independence of the judiciary system, and extortion of private corporations. Any effort to promote public accountability and strengthen the rural communities remains wedded to resolution of the land issue.

In short, in the three countries there are few indications that the voice and influence of the rural poor will increase as a result of the economic reforms. The power of the political insiders and emerging economic elite will determine national development priorities in the foreseeable future.

PURSUING REFORMS WITHOUT A NATIONAL CONSENSUS

Misplaced Policies

Liberalizing the three resource-based economies was imperative if improved living standards were to be achieved. However, pursuing the goal of economic liberalization and reestablishing macroeconomic equilibrium through the strict application of prescripts of the Washington consensus were misplaced on numerous counts.

- First, the international structure of demand and the accompanying declining terms of trade cannot provide the economic foundations for addressing the persistent debt burdens while reversing the deepening grip of poverty on these societies. Regardless of the efficiency gains, introduction of new technology and broadening of market access associated with economic reforms, the resource-based sectors cannot pull the economies out of their current problems.
- Second, replacing state rent-seeking in natural resource sectors with private rent-seeking cannot provide the economic foundations or government revenues for addressing the debt overhang and supporting development priorities. Allowing private, notably foreign, corpo-

rations access to the countries' natural resource wealth under the prevailing economic and institutional conditions could not provide economic returns such that a reversal in economic fortunes was possible.

- Third, the institutional framework for reestablishing macroeconomic equilibrium through the prescribed policy reforms is lacking. The policy prescriptions required complex regulatory and managerial scaffolding absent in these countries. The mechanisms for overseeing the natural resource sectors were not put in place prior to or during the reform process, leaving the countries open to rent seeking and corrupt business practices.

The difficulties of Bretton Woods institutions in responding to the particular political systems of the countries and creating an adequate institutional scaffolding and regulatory framework in which a neoliberal economy could flourish contributed significantly to the setbacks experienced during the reform process. Those factors created repeated uncertainties that led to the frequent flip-flops of the Bretton Woods institutions as they embraced autocrats, then repudiated them, heralded the new democratic regimes, only to lament their ineffectiveness in implementing economic reform programmes. The World Bank and IMF did not understand the particular challenges of addressing the political dynamics of autocratic regimes nor did they adequately address the linkages between those regimes and exploitation of natural resource wealth.

Misplaced Priorities

Coupled with the limitations of the approach pursued by Bretton Woods institutions we must take account of the misplaced priorities of national political leaders. The policy prescriptions of the Washington consensus, successful by some measures in other countries, were proposed to national leaders of the three countries who, to varying degrees, had little or no direct interest in seeing them implemented. By the time that reform programmes were introduced in the late 1980s and early 1990s, variants of socialist policies and nationalist ideologies had run their course, unable to deliver improved standards of living or open new opportunities for the majority of citizens. Those failures notwithstanding, national political elites had vested interests in the maintenance of state-run economies for numerous reasons, among them that their personal economic and political fortunes depended on them. Whatever ideological or moral veneer the ruling elites used to justify their behaviour, economic reforms posed challenges to the prevailing economic order and their own positions of power and privilege in that order.

Hence, these two sets of players, one international and the other national, engaged in a complex battle of power and political will, each trying to open up or maintain control over the natural resource wealth of the countries. Even though many elements of the Bretton Woods institutions' economic reforms have been implemented, respect for them has been undermined and weakened through mechanisms of delay, dilution and corruption at various levels of government. This outcome should not be surprising, nor should the fact that the costs of the often disappointing results have fallen largely on the poor, particularly the rural poor.

A lack of national purpose and consensus consistently eroded implementation of the reforms in each of the countries over the past decade or more. In Zambia, pursuing a cash budget, reestablishing fiscal balance and privatizing the mining sector as required by the Bretton Woods institutions drove national economic policy and became a substitute for a national development strategy. In Zimbabwe, what started out as an effort to strengthen the industrial sector's competitiveness contributed to a larger political crisis and economic collapse as the reform process assumed that it could skirt underlying conflicts over land. In Tanzania, the strictures of the reform package drove the process of structural and societal change without being rooted in a national development strategy endorsed by the broadest sections of the population. A renewed sense of national purpose may eventually emerge from the reform process depending, to a large degree, on the opportunities and material improvements accruing to the rural population.

Missing Factor in the Development Equation

Historically, civil society in countries both North and South often has emerged in response to autocratic regimes and exclusion from political processes and decision making. In equal measure, civil society has grown from capitalism's failure to redistribute the benefits of economic growth equitably. More recently, the economic system's externalization of environmental costs has spawned further expansion of civil society to reverse the weakening of the planet's environmental fabric.

The demands and protests from civil society have altered public policies, economic incentives, regulatory regimes and institutional arrangements on both national and international levels. Such changes have resulted in the establishment of more responsive, accountable systems of governance, wealth redistribution and environmental regulatory regimes. Moreover, where the private sector and government have failed to provide services required for social wellbeing, civil society has often taken on multi-faceted management and service provision functions, including, occasionally, in the three countries covered by these essays.

In those three countries, ruling parties repressed and manipulated civil society in different ways, with varying intensity, and for different purposes over the past decades. During the reform processes, neither multilateral development institutions nor national governments have sought to strengthen the participation of civil society shaping or refining the reform programme. Quite to the contrary, the World Bank and IMF have shielded their policies and agreements from the scrutiny of the affected public, seldom identifying clearly who the 'affected public' was, and less frequently responding to its expressed needs. Moreover, national governments and political elites have used civil society for political purposes when public protests would aid the elites' efforts to fend off the efforts of the Bretton Woods institutions to alter their positions of privilege and power.

Under the repression of political elites and exclusion by the Bretton Woods institutions, groups from civil society have faced innumerable challenges in exercising the necessary watchdog and advocacy functions often taken for granted in more democratic societies. Without those public functions, little has remained to prevent new forms of exclusion, corruption and mismanagement becoming entrenched in emerging economic and political systems.

Over the past decades of economic reform, bilateral development agencies, agencies of the United Nations development system and international non-government organizations have been steady investors seeking to strengthen the voice and influence of non-governmental and community-based organizations. In short, with minor exceptions, civil society has been excluded from the reform process except as a political pawn to be used for the government's political ends.

In its most recent assessment of the adjustment experience in Africa, *Aid and Reform in Africa*, the World Bank emphasizes a lesson it has highlighted many times over the past decade, namely the importance of policy ownership (Devarajan et al 2001). As stated, ownership means 'that there is political commitment to change and able technocrats who can work out the details of reform'. In light of the experiences highlighted in previous chapters, that concept rings empty. For example, political leaders and technocrats in Zambia and Tanzania have accepted the need to embark on structural reform programmes of one form or another. Moreover, political leaders' earlier opposition has now been supplanted by the sense of new opportunity, if not for the country, then certainly for their personal fortunes. Is that the sense of ownership by political leaders and technocrats that the Bank invokes? We have to ask: What about the rest of the population, the rural and urban poor who are carrying the burdens of the adjustment process? What about the sense of a national enterprise, national priorities and a social contract that could coalesce the nation's support for a reform process? This deficient concept of ownership has encouraged reform processes bereft of national consensus and national purpose. That deficient concept of ownership has also encouraged the exclusion of groups from civil society as active participants in the reform process. Ultimately, that concept has also sapped the credibility of national governments, development institutions and the reform process.

By Way of Recommendations

The Bretton Woods Institutions

Many of the recommendations directed to the Bretton Woods institutions in our previous research and advocacy programmes, including the need to establish transitional strategies for allowing the rural poor to adjust to new market conditions, remain as relevant today as years earlier. We will, however, underscore one central issue in this closing section as regards the World Bank and IMF, specifically, implementing strategic analysis and planning instruments for all policy and programmatic lending operations.

In coming years, policy-based lending operations are expected to increase both in number and diversity and will constitute a larger percentage of the Bank's lending portfolio. Standard macroeconomic and sectoral adjustment operations will be accompanied by poverty reduction strategy credits, adaptable programme loans and public expenditure review loans, among others. These lending instruments will focus on providing more flexible lines of credit to deepen economic reform programmes.

Both standard and new programmatic lending fall outside the requirements of environmental assessments established by the World Bank. Such requirements do not pertain to the IMF at all. Despite the fact that some countries have been engaged in such policy reforms for over 15 years, the Bretton Woods institutions have yet to require an assessment of these lending packages on the adjusting countries' social structures or the environment. Correcting this policy failure remains of paramount importance.

One of the outputs of WWF's project in southern Africa was an environmental impact assessment instrument for macroeconomic reform programmes (Iannariello et al 2000). It was designed to encourage the World Bank and IMF to shape the substance and process of future structural adjustment programmes. Regardless of the relative merits and weaknesses of that or any other assessment instrument, what is of particular concern to us here is that all future policy and programmatic lending operations of both the World Bank and IMF be subjected to a comprehensive risk analysis and monitoring procedure. To this end we insist that strategic analysis and planning instruments include four specific features:

1   The strategic analysis and planning instrument must integrate environmental and social considerations into a unified perspective. Economic reforms affect social groups in different ways, altering their status and opportunities, and also altering the ways those groups rely on and interact with the environment. Similarly, economic reforms influence environmental resources in different ways, affecting the livelihoods and opportunities of different social groups. Hence, a seamless integrated strategic impact assessment combining social and environmental effects must frame any policy or programmatic lending operations.

2   The strategic analysis and planning instrument must establish a clear statement of environmental and social risks that are associated with any policy-based operation. That assessment of risk must specify the precise indicators that are to be used to monitor the environmental and social impacts of the reform process.

3   An independent monitoring mechanism must be established alongside government to gauge the environmental and social performance of the policy operations on a regular basis. The functioning of this monitoring mechanism must be accessible to the concerned public and the results of monitoring must likewise be made available to the public on a regular, frequent basis.

4   A policy response mechanism must be established, and authority and responsibility delegated to that body so that appropriate government agencies are empowered to respond to and correct unacceptable costs associated with policy and institutional reforms.

By applying a responsive, publicly accessible assessment instrument to all policy operations, the Bretton Woods institutions can significantly improve the social and environmental outcomes of reform processes. In addition, applying this strategic analysis and monitoring tool could contribute significantly to breaking with their past record of excluding civil society from involvement in policy reforms and provide the mechanisms for strengthening civil society's role vis-à-vis entrenched interest groups.

Strengthening the Role of Civil Society

Our second recommendation concerns the importance of strengthening civil society in developing countries, particularly in countries with resource-based economies. The experiences of these three countries underscore the importance of mechanisms of public oversight and accountability in ensuring that natural resource wealth is used for public, not just private, good. In the absence of watchdog and advocacy activities of a diverse band of civic organizations, public and private rent-seeking finds fertile ground, and collusion between economic and political actors flourishes.

In the light of the above, we strongly recommend expansion of the investments of bilateral agencies, specialized agencies of the UN development system and international NGOs in promoting the development of local community and advocacy groups, be they in the field of governance, development, human rights or the environment, to developing groups from civil society. Specifically, we recommend investment of resources to strengthen the capacity of NGOs in developing countries to monitor and analyse developments and changes in natural resource sectors. Investments should encourage strengthening the public's ability to monitor and be involved in natural resource sectors in the following ways:

- analyse and highlight the role of natural resource wealth in national development plans and strategies;
- identify the corresponding government agencies and government staff responsible for managing main natural resource sectors;
- identify the policy framework and legal mechanisms that regulate economic activity in those sectors;
- monitor proposed institutional changes in those sectors, including land reform, resource authorities and decentralization proposals, among others;

- analyse, whenever possible, the linkages between economic agents active in the resource sectors and government employees and policy makers; and
- develop policy and institutional proposals designed to increase local control over resources and revenues derived from those resources.

We also recommend that bilateral and UN development agencies, along with international NGOs, provide resources so that local organizations can establish information-sharing mechanisms with other NGOs and stakeholders around the world.

Guiding Principles: Natural Resource Wealth and the Rural Poor

The foregoing conclusions highlight a unique set of issues particular to natural resource-based economies that need to be addressed if democratic regimes are to take firm root and if sustainable development paths are to drive national development strategies. They highlight the fact that economic changes in countries of sub-Saharan Africa are unfolding in ways that create many opportunities for the entrepreneurial classes and those with political influence. The conclusions also underscore the point that creation of opportunities for the more competitive companies and individuals is accompanied by a sense among the poor, particularly the rural poor, of continued loss of economic control and disempowerment in the political sphere. That growing vulnerability is expressed both through exclusion and marginalization as well as through material loss in conflicts with more powerful economic agents and political actors.

As an international environmental organization, WWF's abiding interest is in promoting conservation and the sustainable management of our planet's natural resource base. Given the rural character of these investments, notably in frontier and rural areas of rich biodiversity, we have worked consistently with rural communities to find ways of addressing their needs to improve livelihoods and our conservation agenda. One of the main lessons learned from decades of investment in developing countries is that conservation objectives can best be fulfilled if people living in rural areas enjoy stable, productive lives. Stated in other terms, poverty alleviation and conservation must go hand in hand, and we must find ways of addressing those two concerns in a harmonious, mutually supportive way.

WWF remains far from having found formulaic answers to the complex dynamic linking rural poverty, conservation and natural resource wealth. As with other environmental and development organizations, WWF is steadily challenged to explore new approaches to addressing these dynamics, particularly today as new economic incentives and institutional reforms associated with the neoliberal economic regime increase pressure on fragile rural areas. What is certain, however, is that the neoliberal policies and accompanying institutional reforms are carrying us no closer to addressing the complex dynamic between rural poverty and the environment.

The transition to market-based economies in countries of sub-Saharan Africa is not only necessary but also urgent. However, a new set of principles governing changes in rural areas must be implemented if more favourable poverty alleviation and conservation outcomes are to be accomplished. The thrust of those principles is to strengthen the control of the rural poor over environmental assets and natural resource wealth and to provide sustained inputs and support such that the rural poor can use those resources more productively and sustainably. To that end the following principles serve as the basis for establishing economic and institutional policy in the rural areas of developing countries.

- Protecting the access of the rural poor to environmental resources. This principle recognizes the increased threats to the ability of the rural poor to control environmental assets as a result of neoliberal economic reforms. Every effort must be made to reverse this trend by identifying policies, institutional arrangements and economic incentives that currently work against the rural poor's control of productive assets and converting them into arrangements that strengthen the rural poor.
- Expanding the control over and access of the rural poor to environmental resources. This principle grows from recognition that unless the productive assets of the poor expand, alleviation of rural poverty

will remain a distant aspiration for hundreds of millions of rural citizens.

- Redistributing revenues derived from natural resources to the rural poor. Governments need to establish fiscal policies and redistribution mechanisms to ensure that a stable, steady flow of natural resource revenues is channelled to local communities. This principle is designed to guarantee that fiscal policies generate a positive resource flow to rural areas, not the inverse, as is currently the case. Moreover, this principle is designed to reverse the prevailing subsidy structure that most frequently favours the non-poor and urban populations.

- Increasing redistribution of revenues from private companies to rural communities. Private companies operating in natural resource sectors should be required to redistribute an established percentage of profits to local communities. This principle is intended to increase the responsibility of both foreign and national corporations for the social development of rural communities where economic activities take place. Moreover, this principle is designed to establish direct interactions between communities and the private sector that depends on a healthy workforce and healthy environmental conditions.

- Establishing co-management arrangements. Co-management regimes for natural resources should be established and broadened between private companies, the state and rural communities. As competition grows among these actors in rural areas, this principle is designed to increase both the economic opportunities as well as the managerial capacities of villagers and their leaders in areas where different groups may have competing interests. For example, co-management arrangements in Zimbabwe (CAMPFIRE) and Zambia (ADMADE) should be reformed and broadened, and the voice and technical capacity of villagers and their representatives should be strengthened.

- Providing supporting inputs to rural producers. Other inputs and targeted supports should be extended to rural producers. The ability to increase productivity in rural areas and the ability to manage resources sustainably require the provision of other inputs and support from government. Those inputs include provision of credit, extension of infrastructure, technical and marketing support and other education over a sustained period of time.

These principles arise from the specific experiences of the three countries considered in this publication. Other principles, particularly regarding governance and human rights, must accompany those suggested above to create a full complement of guiding principles that should, we believe, condition the development of the emerging economic order. This essay concludes, therefore, with a call to the growing number of environmental, human rights and development groups to reach beyond our particular institutional agendas and to agree on common principles that will guide our efforts to place the economic system under greater public scrutiny and to ensure that private sector expansion serves socially-agreed purposes. The foundation of those principles must be to address the economic needs of the rural poor and the need to manage the environment and natural resource wealth sustainably.

Notes and References

INTRODUCTION

Notes

1 David Reed (ed), 1992, *Structural Adjustment and the Environment*, London, Earthscan; David Reed (ed), 1996, *Structural Adjustment, the Environment and Sustainable Development*, London, Earthscan.

2 See, for example, World Bank, 1994, *Economywide Policies and the Environment: Emerging Lessons from Experience*, Washington, DC, World Bank.

3 Those agencies included the European Commission (DG Development), Swedish International Development Agency (Sida), Canadian International Development Agency (CIDA), Swiss Development Corporation (SDC), Bundesministerium für wirtschaftliche Zusammenarbeit und Entwicklung (BMZ), Deutsche Gesellschaft für Technische Zusammenarbeit (GTZ) and Danish International Development Agency (Danida).

4 Research outputs can be obtained from project partners as follows: South Africa, Development Bank of Southern Africa: *WWF Synthesis Report: The Water Sector* and *WWF Synthesis Report: Energy Sector*; Tanzania, Economics Research Bureau of the University of Dar es Salaam: *Macroeconomic Reforms, Mining, and Sustainable Development in Tanzania* and *Macroeconomic Reforms, Tourism, and Sustainable Development in Tanzania*; Zambia, Mano: *Structural Adjustment, Rural Livelihoods and Sustainable Development*; Zimbabwe, ZERO: *Macroeconomic Reforms, Tourism and Sustainable Development*.

5 Although South Africa was included in the four-country project, the highly technical nature of the research and advocacy activities carried out in that

country by the DBSA rendered inclusion of the work in this publication problematic. That is not to say that South Africa has escaped the authoritarianism of the apartheid regime and difficult choices regarding the use of natural resource wealth. On the contrary, the country continues to wrestle with the trade-offs associated with apartheid's legacy by which difficult choices must be made between the pursuit of economic efficiency, distributional equity and environmental sustainability. Use of the country's natural resource wealth will play a major role in facilitating, or impeding, the country's transition to a more equitable society.

CHAPTER 1

Notes

1   Neoliberal economic policy refers to economic policy reforms designed to reduce the economic functions of the state, open statist economies to the flow of capital and goods across borders, and reform the state and its many institutions such that they become subordinate to the needs of the market.

References

Akiyama, Takamsa, John Baffes, Donald Larson and Panayotis Varangis, 2001, *Commodity Market Reforms: Lessons of Two Decades*, Washington, DC, World Bank.

Bangura, Yusuf, 1992, 'Authoritarian Rule and Democracy in Africa: A Theoretical Discourse', in *Authoritarianism, Democracy, and Adjustment: The Politics of Economic Reform in Africa*, Uppsala, Sweden, The Scandinavian Institute of African Studies.

Bangura, Yusuf and Peter Gibbon, 1992, 'Adjustment, Authoritarianism and Democracy', in *Authoritarianism, Democracy, and Adjustment: The Politics of Economic Reform in Africa*, Uppsala, Sweden, The Scandinavian Institute of African Studies.

Booth, Anne, W J O'Malley and Anna Weidermann, 1990, *Indonesian Economic History in the Dutch Colonial Era*, New Haven, Connecticut, Yale University Southeast Asia Studies.

Borensztein, Eduardo, Mohsin S Khan, Carmen M Reinhart and Peter Wickham, 1994, *The Behavior of Non-Oil Commodity Prices*, Washington, DC, International Monetary Fund.

Bratton, Michael, 1994, 'Economic Crisis and Political Realignment in Zambia', in Widner, *Economic Change and Political Liberalization in Sub-Saharan Africa*, Baltimore, Johns Hopkins University Press.

Brett, E A, 1973, *Colonialism and Underdevelopment in East Africa: The Politics of Economic Change, 1919–1939*, Hampshire, England, Gregg Revivals.

Camdessus, M, 1999, quoted in *IMF Survey*, vol 28, no 1, Washington, DC, International Monetary Fund.

Collins, Robert, 1996, *Historical Problems of Imperial Africa*, Princeton, Markus Wiener Publishers.

Comeliau, Christian, 1991, *Les Relations Nord-Sud*, Paris, Éditions La Découverte.

Comeliau, Christian, 1998, 'L'État Subordonné', in *La Pensée Comptable*, Paris, PUF.

Darwin, John, 1988, *Britain and Decolonization: The Retreat from Empire in the Post-War World*, London.

Davis, Lance E and Robert Huttenback, 1986, *Mammon and the Pursuit of Empire: The Political Economy of British Imperialism, 1860–1912*, New York, Cambridge University Press.

Ghai, D, 1991, *The IMF and the South: The Social Impact of Crisis and Adjustment*, London, Zed Books.

Gibbon, Peter, Yusuf Bangura and Arve Ofstad, 1991, *Authoritarianism, Democracy and Adjustment*, Uppsala, Sweden, The Scandinavian Institute of African Studies.

Gibbon, Peter, 1992, 'Structural Adjustment and Pressures Towards Multipartyism in Sub-Saharan Africa', in *Authoritarianism, Democracy and Adjustment: The Politics of Economic Reform in Africa*, Uppsala, Sweden, The Scandinavian Institute of African Studies.

Gibbon, Peter, 1995a, *Liberalized Developing in Tanzania*, Uppsala, Sweden, The Scandinavian Institute of Africa Studies.

Gibbon, Peter (ed), 1995b, *Structural Adjustment and the Working Poor in Zimbabwe*, Uppsala, Sweden, The Scandinavian Institute of African Studies.

Gulhati, Ravi, 1989, *Impasse in Zambia: The Economics and Politics of Reform*, Washington, DC, World Bank.

Havinden, Michael and David Meredith, 1993, *Colonialism and Development*, New York, Routledge.

Hochschild, Adam, 1999, *King Leopold's Ghost*, New York, Houghton Mifflin.

Leite, Carlos, and Jens Weidmann, 1999, *Does Mother Nature Corrupt? Natural Resources, Corruption, and Economic Growth*, Washington, DC, International Monetary Fund.

Louis, William Roger, 1977, *Imperialism at Bay 1941–1945: The United States and the Decolonisation of the British Empire*, London, Oxford University Press.

Maddox, Gregory (ed), 1993, *The Colonial Epoch in Africa*, New York, Garland Publishing.

Mosley, Paul, 1983, *The Settler Economies: Studies in the Economic History of Kenya and Southern Rhodesia 1900–1963*, Cambridge, Cambridge University Press.

Mosley, John, Jane Harrigan and John Toye, 1991, *Aid and Power*, London, Routledge.

Mpuku, Herrick and Ivan Zyuulu, 1997, *Contemporary Issues in Socio-economic Reform in Zambia*, Brookfield, US, Ashgate.

Nelson, Joan, (ed), 1989, *Fragile Coalitions: The Politics of Economic Adjustment*, Washington, DC, Overseas Development Council.

Oliver, Roland and Anthony Atmore, 1967, *Africa Since 1800*, New York, Cambridge University Press.

Pakenham, Thomas, *The Scramble for Africa*, 1991, New York, Avon Press.

Reed, David, 2001, *Poverty is Not a Number, The Environment is Not a Butterfly*, Washington, DC, WWF.

Reed, David (ed), 1996, *Structural Adjustment, the Environment and Sustainable Development*, London, Earthscan.

Rodney, Walter, 1982, *How Europe Underdeveloped Africa*, Washington, DC, Howard University Press.

Sandbrook, Richard, 1985, *The Politics of Africa's Economic Stagnation*, Cambridge, Cambridge University Press.

Skälnes, Tor, 1995, *The Politics of Economic Reform in Zimbabwe*, New York, St Martin's Press.

Stern, Ernie, 1991, 'Evolution and Lessons of Adjustment Lending', in Vinod Thomas et al (eds), *Restructuring Economies in Distress*, Washington, DC, World Bank.

Thomas, Vinod, Ajay Chibber, Mansoor Dailami and Jaime de Melo (eds), 1991, *Restructuring Economies in Distress*, New York, Oxford University Press.

Toye, John, 1992, 'Interest Group Politics and the Implementation of Adjustment Policies in Sub-Saharan Africa', in *Authoritarianism, Democracy, and*

Adjustment: The Politics of Economic Reform in Africa, Uppsala, Sweden, The Scandinavian Institute of African Studies.

Van Der Hoeven, Rolph and Fred Van Der Kraaij, 1994, *Structural Adjustment and Beyond in Sub-Saharan Africa*, Portsmouth, Heinemann.

Wesseling, H L, 1997, *Imperialism and Colonialism, Essays on the History of European Expansion*, London, Greenwood Press.

Widner, Jennifer, 1994, *Economic Change and Political Liberalization in Sub-Saharan Africa*, Baltimore, Johns Hopkins University Press.

Williamson, John (ed), 1994, *The Political Economy of Policy Reform*, Washington, DC, Institute for International Economics.

Wolpert, Stanley, 1989, *A New History of India*, New York, Oxford University Press.

World Bank, 1989, *Sub-Saharan Africa, From Crisis to Sustainable Growth*, Washington, DC.

World Bank, 1994, *Adjustment in Africa*, Washington, DC.

World Bank, 1999, *Global Commodity Markets*, Washington, DC.

World Bank, 2000, *World Development Indicators Database*, Washington, DC.

CHAPTER 2

References

Bagachwa, M S D and Festus Limbu, 1995, *Policy Reform and the Environment in Tanzania*, Dar es Salaam, University of Dar es Salaam.

Baregu, Mwesiga, 1994, 'The Rise and Fall of the One-Party State in Tanzania', in Jennifer Widner (ed), *Economic Change and Political Liberalization in Sub-Saharan Africa*, Baltimore, Johns Hopkins University Press.

Bigsten, Arne, 1999, *Aid and Reform in Tanzania*, Dar es Salaam, Economic and Social Research Foundation.

Bienen, Henry, 1978, *Armies and Parties in Africa*, New York, African Publishing Company.

Bol, Dirk, 1995, 'Winners and Losers of Trade Liberalisation', in M S D Bagachwa and Festus Limbu (eds), 1995, *Policy Reform and the Environment in Tanzania*, Dar es Salaam, Dar es Salaam University Press.

Bol, Dirk, Nathanael Luvanga and Joseph Shitunda, 1997, *Economic Management in Tanzania*, Dar es Salaam, University of Dar es Salaam.

Chachage, S S C, M Ericsson and Peter Gibbon, 1993, *Mining and Structural Adjustment: Studies on Zimbabwe and Tanzania*, Uppsala, Sweden, Scandinavian Institute of African Studies.

Chachage, S L, 1995, 'The Meek Shall Inherit the Earth but Not the Mining Rights', in Peter Gibbon (ed), *Liberalised Development in Tanzania*, Uppsala, Sweden, Nordiska Afrikainstitutet.

Gibbon, Peter (ed), 1995, *Liberalised Development in Tanzania*, Uppsala, Sweden, Nordiska Africkainstitutet.

Kulindwa, Kassim, Oswald Mashindano, Hussein Sosovele and Fanuel Shechambo, 2000a, *Macroeconomic Reforms, Mining, and Sustainable Development in Tanzania*, Dar es Salaam, University of Dar es Salaam.

Kulindwa, Kassim, Oswald Mashindano and Hussein Sosovele, 2000b, *Macroeconomic Reforms, Tourism, and Sustainable Development in Tanzania*, Dar es Salaam, University of Dar es Salaam.

Msambichaka, Lucian, Humphrey Moshi and Fidelis Mtatififolo (eds), 1994, *Development Challenges and Strategies for Tanzania*, Dar es Salaam, University of Dar es Salaam.

Msambichaka, Lucian, A A L Kilindo and G D Mjema, 1995, *Beyond Structural Adjustment Program in Tanzania*, Dar es Salaam, University of Dar es Salaam.

Sarris, Alexander and Rogier Van den Brink, 1994, 'From Forced Modernization to Perestroika: Crisis and Adjustment in Tanzania', in David Sahn (ed), *Adjusting to Policy Failure in African Economies*, Ithaca, Cornell University.

Shechambo, F and Kassim Kulindwa, 1995, 'Environmental Implications of Economic Reform Policies for Agricultural Development in Tanzania', in M S D Bagachwa and Festus Limbu, *Policy Reform and the Environment in Tanzania*, Dar es Salaam, Dar es Salaam University Press.

URT (United Republic of Tanzania), 2000, *A Study on Tourism Earnings in Tanzania*, Dar es Salaam, Ministry of Natural Resources and Tourism.

URT (United Republic of Tanzania), 1996, *Parastatal Sector Reform Commission*, Dar es Salaam.

Van Arkadie, Brian, 1995, 'Economic Strategy and Structural Adjustment in Tanzania', Private Sector Development Department, Occasional Paper No 18, Washington, DC, World Bank.

Weaver, James and Arne Anderson, 1981, 'Stabilization and Development of the Tanzanian Economy in the 1970s', in William Cline and Sidney Weintraub (eds) *Economic Stabilization in Developing Countries*, Washington, DC, The Brookings Institute.

World Bank, 1995, *Tanzania Agriculture: A Joint Study by the Government of Tanzania and the World Bank*, Washington, DC, World Bank.

World Bank, 1996, *Tanzania – The Challenge of Reforms: Growth, Incomes and Welfare*, Washington, DC.

World Bank, 1997a, *Tanzania – Country Assistance Strategy*, Washington, DC.

World Bank, 1997b, *Tanzania – Structural Adjustment Credit Project*, Washington, DC.

CHAPTER 3

References

Bratton, Michael, 1994, 'Economic Crisis and Political Realignment in Zambia', in Jennifer Widner (ed), *Economic Change and Political Liberalization in Sub-Saharan Africa*, Baltimore, Johns Hopkins University Press.

Bratton, Michael and Nicolas van de Walle, 1992, 'Popular Protest and Reform in Africa', *Comparative Politics*, Vol 24, No 4.

Burnell, Peter, 1999, *Taking Stock of Democracy in Zambia*, unpublished document.

Callaghy, Thomas, 1990, 'Lost Between State and Market: The Politics of Economic Adjustment in Ghana, Zambia, and Nigeria', in Joan Nelson (ed), *Economic Crisis and Policy Choice*, Princeton, Princeton University Press.

de Janvry, Alain, 1981, *The Agrarian Question and Reformism in Latin America*, Baltimore, Johns Hopkins University Press.

Devarajan, Shantayanan, David Dollar and Torgny Holmgren, 2001, *Aid and Reform in Africa*, Washington, DC, World Bank.

Economist Intelligence Unit, 1999–2000, *Zambia Country Report*, London, Economist Intelligence Unit.

Engberg-Pedersen, Poul, 1995, *Limits of Adjustment in Africa: The Effects of Economic Liberalisation*, London, Zed Books.

Institute of Development Studies, 1994, *Consultancy on Poverty Assessment and Public Expenditure Issues*, Sussex, University of Sussex.

Gulhati, R, 1989, *Impasse in Zambia: The Economics and Politics of Reform*, Washington, DC, World Bank.

Henderson, Ian, 1993, 'The Origins of Nationalism in East and Central Africa: The Zambian Case', in Gregory Maddox (ed), *The Colonial Epoch in Africa*, New York, Garland Publishing.

International Monetary Fund, 1997, *Zambia – Selected Issues and Statistical Appendix*, Washington, DC, IMF.

Kabimba, M Wynter, 1999, *Lands Act No 29 of 1995*, Lusaka, Mano Consultancy.

Kambenja, Amos, 1996, 'Land Tenure and Economic Development in Zambia', in Herrick Mpuku and Ivan Zyuula (eds), *Contemporary Issues in Socio-Economic Reform in Zambia*, Hampshire, England, Ashgate Publishing Limited.

Kambenja, Amos, 1997, 'Land Tenure and Economic Development in Zambia', in Herrick Mpuku and Ivan Zyuulu, *Contemporary Issues in Socio-economic Reform in Zambia*, Brookfield, USA, Ashgate.

Mano, 2000, *Land Tenure in Zambia: a Historical Perspective*, Lusaka, Mano Consultancy.

Oliver, Roland and Anthony Atmore, 1967, *Africa Since 1800*, New York, Cambridge University Press.

Oliver, Roland and Anthony Atmore, 1994, *Africa Since 1800*, Fourth Edition, Cambridge, Cambridge University Press.

Rakner, Lise, Nicolas van de Walle and Dominic Mulaisho, 1999, 'Aid and Reform in Zambia', in *Aid and Reform in Africa*, Washington, DC, World Bank.

Van de Walle, Nicolas, 'Economic Reform in a Democratizing Africa', in *Comparative Politics*, October, 1999.

World Bank, 1991, *Economic Recovery Credit*, Washington, DC, World Bank.

World Bank, *Privatization and Industrial Reform Adjustment Credit*, Washington, DC, World Bank.

World Bank, 1992, *Zambia: Agricultural Marketing and Processing Infrastructure Project*, Washington, DC, World Bank.

World Bank, 1996a, *Country Assistance Strategy for the Republic of Zambia*, Washington, DC, World Bank.

World Bank, 1996b, *Prospects for Sustainable Growth*, Washington, DC, World Bank.

Chapter 4

References

Akwabi-Ameyaw, Kofi, 1997, 'Producer Cooperative Resettlement Projects in Zimbabwe: Lessons from a Failed Agricultural Development Strategy', in *World Development*, Vol 25, No 3, London.

Bond, Ivan, 1997, *Tourism and Sport Hunting in Zimbabwe: A Summary of Current Status, Potential and Constraints*, Harare, WWF Programme Office.

Economist Intelligence Unit, 1998–2000, *Zimbabwe Country Report*, London, Economist Intelligence Unit.

Gibbon, Peter (ed), 1995, *Structural Adjustment and the Working Poor in Zimbabwe*, Uppsala, Sweden, Nordiska Afrikainstitutet.

Jenkins, Carolyn, 1997, 'The Politics of Economic Policy-Making in Zimbabwe', in *The Journal of Modern Africa Studies*, Cambridge, Cambridge University Press.

Mandondo, Alois, 2000, *Forging (Un)Democratic Resource Governance Systems from the Relic of Zimbabwe's Colonial Past*, forthcoming, Harare.

Mosley, Paul, 1983, *The Settler Economies: Studies in the Economic History of Kenya and Southern Rhodesia 1900–1963*, Cambridge, Cambridge University Press.

Moyo, Sam (ed), 1991, *Zimbabwe's Environmental Dilemma: Balancing Resource Inequalities*, Harare, ZERO.

Moyo, Sam, 1995, *The Land Question in Zimbabwe*, Harare, SAPES.

Moyo, Sam, 2000, *Land Reform under Structural Adjustment in Zimbabwe*, Uppsala, Sweden, Nordiska Afrikainstitutet.

Murphee, Marshall W, 2001, 'Community, Council and Client: A Case Study in Ecotourism Development from Mahenye, Zimbabwe', in D Hulme and M Murphee (eds), *African Wildlife and Livelihoods. The Promise and Performance of Community Conservation*, Oxford, James Currey.

Nhira, Calvin, Sibongile Baker, Peter Gondo, J J Mangono and Crispen Marunda (eds), 1998, *Contesting Inequality in Access to Forests*, London, IIED.

Scoones, I and F Matose, 1995, 'Local Woodland Management: Constraints and Opportunities for Sustainable Resource Use', in *Living with Trees: Policies for Woodland Management in Zimbabwe*, Washington. DC, World Bank.

Skälnes, Tor, 1995, *The Politics of Economic Reform in Zimbabwe*, New York, St Martin's Press.

World Bank, 1991, *Structural Adjustment Program for the Republic of Zimbabwe*, Washington, DC, World Bank.

World Bank, 1995a, *Zimbabwe: Achieving Shared Growth Country Economic Memorandum*, Washington, DC, World Bank.

World Bank, 1995b, *Project Completion Report: Zimbabwe Structural Adjustment Program*, Washington, DC, World Bank.

World Bank, 1997, *Zimbabwe Country Assistance Strategy*, Washington, DC, World Bank.

ZERO, 2000, *Zimbabwe: Macroeconomic Reforms, Tourism and Sustainable Development*, Harare, ZERO.

CONCLUSIONS

References

Devarajan, Shantayanan, David Dollar and Torgny Holmgren, 2001, *Aid and Reform in Africa*, Washington, DC, World Bank.

Iannariello, Maria Pia, Pamela Stedman-Edwards, Robert Blair and David Reed, 2000, *Environmental Impact of Macroeconomic Reform Programs*, Washington, DC, WWF.

Index